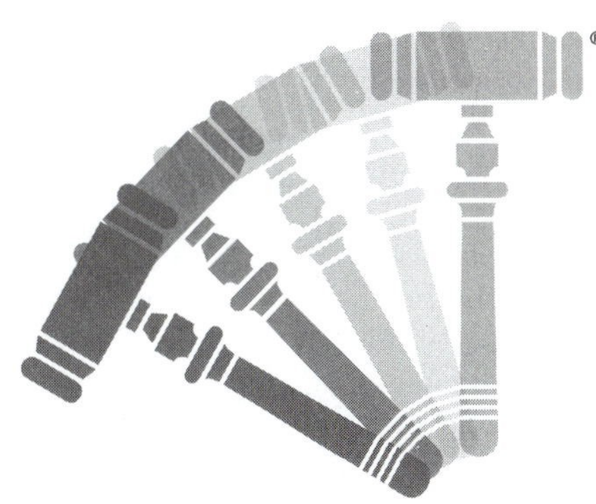

Casenote® Legal Briefs

INTERNATIONAL LAW

Keyed to Courses Using

Carter and Weiner

International Law

Sixth Edition

www.wolterskluwerlb.com

Published by Wolters Kluwer Law & Business in New York.

Wolters Kluwer Law & Business serves customers worldwide with CCH, Aspen Publishers, and Kluwer Law International products.

To contact Customer Service, e-mail customer.service@wolterskluwer.com, call 1-800-234-1660, fax 1-800-901-9075, or mail correspondence to:

Wolters Kluwer Law & Business
Attn: Order Department
P.O. Box 990
Frederick, MD 21705

Printed in the United States of America.

1 2 3 4 5 6 7 8 9 0

ISBN 978-0-7355-9915-4

About Wolters Kluwer Law & Business

Wolters Kluwer Law & Business is a leading global provider of intelligent information and digital solutions for legal and business professionals in key specialty areas, and respected educational resources for professors and law students. Wolters Kluwer Law & Business connects legal and business professionals as well as those in the education market with timely, specialized authoritative content and information-enabled solutions to support success through productivity, accuracy and mobility.

Serving customers worldwide, Wolters Kluwer Law & Business products include those under the Aspen Publishers, CCH, Kluwer Law International, Loislaw, Best Case, ftwilliam.com and MediRegs family of products.

CCH products have been a trusted resource since 1913, and are highly regarded resources for legal, securities, antitrust and trade regulation, government contracting, banking, pension, payroll, employment and labor, and healthcare reimbursement and compliance professionals.

Aspen Publishers products provide essential information to attorneys, business professionals and law students. Written by preeminent authorities, the product line offers analytical and practical information in a range of specialty practice areas from securities law and intellectual property to mergers and acquisitions and pension/benefits. Aspen's trusted legal education resources provide professors and students with high-quality, up-to-date and effective resources for successful instruction and study in all areas of the law.

Kluwer Law International products provide the global business community with reliable international legal information in English. Legal practitioners, corporate counsel and business executives around the world rely on Kluwer Law journals, looseleafs, books, and electronic products for comprehensive information in many areas of international legal practice.

Loislaw is a comprehensive online legal research product providing legal content to law firm practitioners of various specializations. Loislaw provides attorneys with the ability to quickly and efficiently find the necessary legal information they need, when and where they need it, by facilitating access to primary law as well as state-specific law, records, forms and treatises.

Best Case Solutions is the leading bankruptcy software product to the bankruptcy industry. It provides software and workflow tools to flawlessly streamline petition preparation and the electronic filing process, while timely incorporating ever-changing court requirements.

ftwilliam.com offers employee benefits professionals the highest quality plan documents (retirement, welfare and non-qualified) and government forms (5500/PBGC, 1099 and IRS) software at highly competitive prices.

MediRegs products provide integrated health care compliance content and software solutions for professionals in healthcare, higher education and life sciences, including professionals in accounting, law and consulting.

Wolters Kluwer Law & Business, a division of Wolters Kluwer, is headquartered in New York. Wolters Kluwer is a market-leading global information services company focused on professionals.

Format for the Casenote® Legal Brief

Nature of Case: This section identifies the form of action (e.g., breach of contract, negligence, battery), the type of proceeding (e.g., demurrer, appeal from trial court's jury instructions), or the relief sought (e.g., damages, injunction, criminal sanctions).

Party ID: Quick identification of the relationship between the parties.

Fact Summary: This is included to refresh your memory and can be used as a quick reminder of the facts.

Rule of Law: Summarizes the general principle of law that the case illustrates. It may be used for instant recall of the court's holding and for classroom discussion or home review.

Facts: This section contains all relevant facts of the case, including the contentions of the parties and the lower court holdings. It is written in a logical order to give the student a clear understanding of the case. The plaintiff and defendant are identified by their proper names throughout and are always labeled with a (P) or (D).

Palsgraf v. Long Island R.R. Co.

Injured bystander (P) v. Railroad company (D)

N.Y. Ct. App., 248 N.Y. 339, 162 N.E. 99 (1928).

NATURE OF CASE: Appeal from judgment affirming verdict for plaintiff seeking damages for personal injury.

FACT SUMMARY: Helen Palsgraf (P) was injured on R.R.'s (D) train platform when R.R.'s (D) guard helped a passenger aboard a moving train, causing his package to fall on the tracks. The package contained fireworks which exploded, creating a shock that tipped a scale onto Palsgraf (P).

RULE OF LAW
The risk reasonably to be perceived defines the duty to be obeyed.

FACTS: Helen Palsgraf (P) purchased a ticket to Rockaway Beach from R.R. (D) and was waiting on the train platform. As she waited, two men ran to catch a train that was pulling out from the platform. The first man jumped aboard, but the second man, who appeared as if he might fall, was helped aboard by the guard on the train who had kept the door open so they could jump aboard. A guard on the platform also helped by pushing him onto the train. The man was carrying a package wrapped in newspaper. In the process, the man dropped his package, which fell on the tracks. The package contained fireworks and exploded. The shock of the explosion was apparently of great enough strength to tip over some scales at the other end of the platform, which fell on Palsgraf (P) and injured her. A jury awarded her damages, and R.R. (D) appealed.

ISSUE: Does the risk reasonably to be perceived define the duty to be obeyed?

HOLDING AND DECISION: (Cardozo, C.J.) Yes. The risk reasonably to be perceived defines the duty to be obeyed. If there is no foreseeable hazard to the injured party as the result of a seemingly innocent act, the act does not become a tort because it happened to be a wrong as to another. If the wrong was not willful, the plaintiff must show that the act as to her had such great and apparent possibilities of danger as to entitle her to protection. Negligence in the abstract is not enough upon which to base liability. Negligence is a relative concept, evolving out of the common law doctrine of trespass on the case. To establish liability, the defendant must owe a legal duty of reasonable care to the injured party. A cause of action in tort will lie where harm, though unintended, could have been averted or avoided by observance of such a duty. The scope of the duty is limited by the range of danger that a reasonable person could foresee. In this case, there was nothing to suggest from the appearance of the parcel or otherwise that the parcel contained fireworks. The guard could not reasonably have had any warning of a threat to Palsgraf (P), and R.R. (D) therefore cannot be held liable. Judgment is reversed in favor of R.R. (D).

DISSENT: (Andrews, J.) The concept that there is no negligence unless R.R. (D) owes a legal duty to take care as to Palsgraf (P) herself is too narrow. Everyone owes to the world at large the duty of refraining from those acts that may unreasonably threaten the safety of others. If the guard's action was negligent as to those nearby, it was also negligent as to those outside what might be termed the "danger zone." For Palsgraf (P) to recover, R.R.'s (D) negligence must have been the proximate cause of her injury, a question of fact for the jury.

ANALYSIS

The majority defined the limit of the defendant's liability in terms of the danger that a reasonable person in defendant's situation would have perceived. The dissent argued that the limitation should not be placed on liability, but rather on damages. Judge Andrews suggested that only injuries that would not have happened but for R.R.'s (D) negligence should be compensable. Both the majority and dissent recognized the policy-driven need to limit liability for negligent acts, seeking, in the words of Judge Andrews, to define a framework "that will be practical and in keeping with the general understanding of mankind." The Restatement (Second) of Torts has accepted Judge Cardozo's view.

Quicknotes

FORESEEABILITY A reasonable expectation that change is the probable result of certain acts or omissions.

NEGLIGENCE Conduct falling below the standard of care that a reasonable person would demonstrate under similar conditions.

PROXIMATE CAUSE The natural sequence of events without which an injury would not have been sustained.

Concurrence/Dissent: All concurrences and dissents are briefed whenever they are included by the casebook editor.

Analysis: This last paragraph gives you a broad understanding of where the case "fits in" with other cases in the section of the book and with the entire course. It is a hornbook-style discussion indicating whether the case is a majority or minority opinion and comparing the principal case with other cases in the casebook. It may also provide analysis from restatements, uniform codes, and law review articles. The analysis will prove to be invaluable to classroom discussion.

Issue: The issue is a concise question that brings out the essence of the opinion as it relates to the section of the casebook in which the case appears. Both substantive and procedural issues are included if relevant to the decision.

Holding and Decision: This section offers a clear and in-depth discussion of the rule of the case and the court's rationale. It is written in easy-to-understand language and answers the issue presented by applying the law to the facts of the case. When relevant, it includes a thorough discussion of the exceptions to the case as listed by the court, any major cites to the other cases on point, and the names of the judges who wrote the decisions.

Quicknotes: Conveniently defines legal terms found in the case and summarizes the nature of any statutes, codes, or rules referred to in the text.

Note to Students

Wolters Kluwer Law & Business is proud to offer *Casenote® Legal Briefs*—continuing thirty years of publishing America's best-selling legal briefs.

Casenote® Legal Briefs are designed to help you save time when briefing assigned cases. Organized under convenient headings, they show you how to abstract the basic facts and holdings from the text of the actual opinions handed down by the courts. Used as part of a rigorous study regimen, they can help you spend more time analyzing and critiquing points of law than on copying bits and pieces of judicial opinions into your notebook or outline.

Casenote® Legal Briefs should never be used as a substitute for assigned casebook readings. They work best when read as a follow-up to reviewing the underlying opinions themselves. Students who try to avoid reading and digesting the judicial opinions in their casebooks or online sources will end up shortchanging themselves in the long run. The ability to absorb, critique, and restate the dynamic and complex elements of case law decisions is crucial to your success in law school and beyond. It cannot be developed vicariously.

Casenote® Legal Briefs represents but one of the many offerings in Legal Education's Study Aid Timeline, which includes:

- *Casenote® Legal Briefs*
- *Emanuel Law Outlines*
- *Examples & Explanations* Series
- *Introduction to Law* Series
- Emanuel *Law in a Flash* Flash Cards
- Emanuel *CrunchTime* Series

Each of these series is designed to provide you with easy-to-understand explanations of complex points of law. Each volume offers guidance on the principles of legal analysis and, consulted regularly, will hone your ability to spot relevant issues. We have titles that will help you prepare for class, prepare for your exams, and enhance your general comprehension of the law along the way.

To find out more about Wolters Kluwer Law & Business' study aid publications, visit us online at *www.wolterskluwerlb.com* or email us at *legaledu@wolterskluwer.com.* We'll be happy to assist you.

Get this Casenote® Legal Brief as an AspenLaw Studydesk eBook today!

By returning this form to Wolters Kluwer Law & Business, you will receive a complimentary eBook download of this Casenote® Legal Brief and AspenLaw Studydesk productivity software.* Learn more about AspenLaw Studydesk today at *www.wolterskluwerlb.com.*

Name		**Phone** ( )
Address		**Apt. No.**
City	**State**	**ZIP Code**
Law School		**Graduation Date** Month ________ Year ________

Cut out the UPC found on the lower left corner of the back cover of this book. Staple the UPC inside this box. Only the original UPC from the book cover will be accepted. (No photocopies or store stickers are allowed.)

Attach UPC inside this box.

Email (Print legibly or you may not get access!)
Title of this book (course subject)
ISBN of this book (10- or 13-digit number on the UPC)
Used with which casebook (provide author's name)

Mail the completed form to:

Wolters Kluwer Law & Business
Legal Education Division
130 Turner Street, Bldg 3, 4th Floor
Waltham, MA 02453-8901

* Upon receipt of this completed form, you will be emailed a code for the digital download of this book in AspenLaw Studydesk eBook format and a free copy of the software application, which is required to read the eBook.

For a full list of eBook study aids available for AspenLaw Studydesk software and other resources that will help you with your law school studies, visit *www.wolterskluwerlb.com.*

Make a photocopy of this form and your UPC for your records.

For detailed information on the use of the information you provide on this form, please see the PRIVACY POLICY at *www.wolterskluwerlb.com.*

How to Brief a Case

A. Decide on a Format and Stick to It

Structure is essential to a good brief. It enables you to arrange systematically the related parts that are scattered throughout most cases, thus making manageable and understandable what might otherwise seem to be an endless and unfathomable sea of information. There are, of course, an unlimited number of formats that can be utilized. However, it is best to find one that suits your needs and stick to it. Consistency breeds both efficiency and the security that when called upon you will know where to look in your brief for the information you are asked to give.

Any format, as long as it presents the essential elements of a case in an organized fashion, can be used. Experience, however, has led *Casenote® Legal Briefs* to develop and utilize the following format because of its logical flow and universal applicability.

NATURE OF CASE: This is a brief statement of the legal character and procedural status of the case (e.g., "Appeal of a burglary conviction").

There are many different alternatives open to a litigant dissatisfied with a court ruling. The key to determining which one has been used is to discover *who is asking this court for what.*

This first entry in the brief should be kept as *short as possible.* Use the court's terminology if you understand it. But since jurisdictions vary as to the titles of pleadings, the best entry is the one that addresses who wants what in this proceeding, not the one that sounds most like the court's language.

RULE OF LAW: A statement of the general principle of law that the case illustrates (e.g., "An acceptance that varies any term of the offer is considered a rejection and counteroffer").

Determining the rule of law of a case is a procedure similar to determining the issue of the case. Avoid being fooled by red herrings; there may be a few rules of law mentioned in the case excerpt, but usually only one is *the* rule with which the casebook editor is concerned. The techniques used to locate the issue, described below, may also be utilized to find the rule of law. Generally, your best guide is simply the chapter heading. It is a clue to the point the casebook editor seeks to make and should be kept in mind when reading every case in the respective section.

FACTS: A synopsis of only the essential facts of the case, i.e., those bearing upon or leading up to the issue.

The facts entry should be a short statement of the events and transactions that led one party to initiate legal proceedings against another in the first place. While some cases conveniently state the salient facts at the beginning of the decision, in other instances they will have to be culled from hiding places throughout the text, even from concurring and dissenting opinions. Some of the "facts" will often be in dispute and should be so noted. Conflicting evidence may be briefly pointed up. "Hard" facts must be included. Both must be *relevant* in order to be listed in the facts entry. It is impossible to tell what is relevant until the entire case is read, as the ultimate determination of the rights and liabilities of the parties may turn on something buried deep in the opinion.

Generally, the facts entry should not be longer than three to five *short* sentences.

It is often helpful to identify the role played by a party in a given context. For example, in a construction contract case the identification of a party as the "contractor" or "builder" alleviates the need to tell that that party was the one who was supposed to have built the house.

It is always helpful, and a good general practice, to identify the "plaintiff" and the "defendant." This may seem elementary and uncomplicated, but, especially in view of the creative editing practiced by some casebook editors, it is sometimes a difficult or even impossible task. Bear in mind that the *party presently* seeking something from this court may not be the plaintiff, and that sometimes only the cross-claim of a defendant is treated in the excerpt. Confusing or misaligning the parties can ruin your analysis and understanding of the case.

ISSUE: A statement of the general legal question answered by or illustrated in the case. For clarity, the issue is best put in the form of a question capable of a "yes" or "no" answer. In reality, the issue is simply the Rule of Law put in the form of a question (e.g., "May an offer be accepted by performance?").

The major problem presented in discerning what is *the* issue in the case is that an opinion usually purports to raise and answer several questions. However, except for rare cases, only one such question is really the issue in the case. Collateral issues not necessary to the resolution of the matter in controversy are handled by the court by language known as *"obiter dictum"* or merely *"dictum."* While dicta may be included later in the brief, they have no place under the issue heading.

To find the issue, ask *who wants what* and then go on to ask *why did that party succeed or fail in getting it.* Once this is determined, the "why" should be turned into a question.

The complexity of the issues in the cases will vary, but in all cases a single-sentence question should sum up the issue. *In a few cases,* there will be two, or even more rarely, three issues of equal importance to the resolution of the case. Each should be expressed in a single-sentence question.

Since many issues are resolved by a court in coming to a final disposition of a case, the casebook editor will reproduce the portion of the opinion containing the issue or issues most relevant to the area of law under scrutiny. A noted law professor gave this advice: "Close the book; look at the title on the cover." Chances are, if it is Property, you need not concern yourself with whether, for example, the federal government's treatment of the plaintiff's land really raises a federal question sufficient to support jurisdiction on this ground in federal court.

The same rule applies to chapter headings designating sub-areas within the subjects. They tip you off as to what the text is designed to teach. The cases are arranged in a casebook to show a progression or development of the law, so that the preceding cases may also help.

It is also most important to remember to *read the notes and questions* at the end of a case to determine what the editors wanted you to have gleaned from it.

HOLDING AND DECISION: This section should succinctly explain the rationale of the court in arriving at its decision. In capsulizing the "reasoning" of the court, it should always include an application of the general rule or rules of law to the specific facts of the case. Hidden justifications come to light in this entry: the reasons for the state of the law, the public policies, the biases and prejudices, those considerations that influence the justices' thinking and, ultimately, the outcome of the case. At the end, there should be a short indication of the disposition or procedural resolution of the case (e.g., "Decision of the trial court for Mr. Smith (P) reversed").

The foregoing format is designed to help you "digest" the reams of case material with which you will be faced in your law school career. Once mastered by practice, it will place at your fingertips the information the authors of your casebooks have sought to impart to you in case-by-case illustration and analysis.

B. Be as Economical as Possible in Briefing Cases

Once armed with a format that encourages succinctness, it is as important to be economical with regard to the time spent on the actual reading of the case as it is to be economical in the writing of the brief itself. This does not mean "skimming" a case. Rather, it means reading the case with an "eye" trained to recognize into which "section" of your brief a particular passage or line fits and having a system for quickly and precisely marking the case so that the passages fitting any one particular part of the brief can be easily identified and brought together in a concise and accurate manner when the brief is actually written.

It is of no use to simply repeat everything in the opinion of the court; record only enough information to trigger your recollection of what the court said. Nevertheless, an accurate statement of the "law of the case," i.e., the legal principle applied to the facts, is absolutely essential to class preparation and to learning the law under the case method.

To that end, it is important to develop a "shorthand" that you can use to make marginal notations. These notations will tell you at a glance in which section of the brief you will be placing that particular passage or portion of the opinion.

Some students prefer to underline all the salient portions of the opinion (with a pencil or colored underliner marker), making marginal notations as they go along. Others prefer the color-coded method of underlining, utilizing different colors of markers to underline the salient portions of the case, each separate color being used to represent a different section of the brief. For example, blue underlining could be used for passages relating to the rule of law, yellow for those relating to the issue, and green for those relating to the holding and decision, etc. While it has its advocates, the color-coded method can be confusing and time-consuming (all that time spent on changing colored markers). Furthermore, it can interfere with the continuity and concentration many students deem essential to the reading of a case for maximum comprehension. In the end, however, it is a matter of personal preference and style. Just remember, whatever method you use, underlining must be used sparingly or its value is lost.

If you take the marginal notation route, an efficient and easy method is to go along underlining the key portions of the case and placing in the margin alongside them the following "markers" to indicate where a particular passage or line "belongs" in the brief you will write:

N (NATURE OF CASE)
RL (RULE OF LAW)
I (ISSUE)
HL (HOLDING AND DECISION, relates to the RULE OF LAW behind the decision)
HR (HOLDING AND DECISION, gives the RATIONALE or reasoning behind the decision)
HA (HOLDING AND DECISION, APPLIES the general principle(s) of law to the facts of the case to arrive at the decision)

Remember that a particular passage may well contain information necessary to more than one part of your brief, in which case you simply note that in the margin. If you are using the color-coded underlining method instead of marginal notation, simply make asterisks or checks in the margin next to the passage in question in the colors that indicate the additional sections of the brief where it might be utilized.

The economy of utilizing "shorthand" in marking cases for briefing can be maintained in the actual brief writing process itself by utilizing "law student shorthand" within the brief. There are many commonly used words and phrases for which abbreviations can be substituted in your briefs (and in your class notes also). You can develop abbreviations that are personal to you and which will save you a lot of time. A reference list of briefing abbreviations can be found on page xii of this book.

C. Use Both the Briefing Process and the Brief as a Learning Tool

Now that you have a format and the tools for briefing cases efficiently, the most important thing is to make the time spent in briefing profitable to you and to make the most advantageous use of the briefs you create. Of course, the briefs are invaluable for classroom reference when you are called upon to explain or analyze a particular case. However, they are also useful in reviewing for exams. A quick glance at the fact summary should bring the case to mind, and a rereading of the rule of law should enable you to go over the underlying legal concept in your mind, how it was applied in that particular case, and how it might apply in other factual settings.

As to the value to be derived from engaging in the briefing process itself, there is an immediate benefit that arises from being forced to sift through the essential facts and reasoning from the court's opinion and to succinctly express them in your own words in your brief. The process ensures that you understand the case and the point that it illustrates, and that means you will be ready to absorb further analysis and information brought forth in class. It also ensures you will have something to say when called upon in class. The briefing process helps develop a mental agility for getting to the *gist* of a case and for identifying, expounding on, and applying the legal concepts and issues found there. The briefing process is the mental process on which you must rely in taking law school examinations; it is also the mental process upon which a lawyer relies in serving his clients and in making his living.

Abbreviations for Briefs

acceptance	acp
affirmed	aff
answer	ans
assumption of risk	a/r
attorney	atty
beyond a reasonable doubt	b/r/d
bona fide purchaser	BFP
breach of contract	br/k
cause of action	c/a
common law	c/l
Constitution	Con
constitutional	con
contract	K
contributory negligence	c/n
cross	x
cross-complaint	x/c
cross-examination	x/ex
cruel and unusual punishment	c/u/p
defendant	D
dismissed	dis
double jeopardy	d/j
due process	d/p
equal protection	e/p
equity	eq
evidence	ev
exclude	exc
exclusionary rule	exc/r
felony	f/n
freedom of speech	f/s
good faith	g/f
habeas corpus	h/c
hearsay	hr
husband	H
injunction	inj
in loco parentis	ILP
inter vivos	I/v
joint tenancy	j/t
judgment	judgt
jurisdiction	jur
last clear chance	LCC
long-arm statute	LAS
majority view	maj
meeting of minds	MOM
minority view	min
Miranda rule	Mir/r
Miranda warnings	Mir/w
negligence	neg
notice	ntc
nuisance	nus
obligation	ob
obscene	obs
offer	O
offeree	OE
offeror	OR
ordinance	ord
pain and suffering	p/s
parol evidence	p/e
plaintiff	P
prima facie	p/f
probable cause	p/c
proximate cause	px/c
real property	r/p
reasonable doubt	r/d
reasonable man	r/m
rebuttable presumption	rb/p
remanded	rem
res ipsa loquitur	RIL
respondeat superior	r/s
Restatement	RS
reversed	rev
Rule Against Perpetuities	RAP
search and seizure	s/s
search warrant	s/w
self-defense	s/d
specific performance	s/p
statute	S
statute of frauds	S/F
statute of limitations	S/L
summary judgment	s/j
tenancy at will	t/w
tenancy in common	t/c
tenant	t
third party	TP
third party beneficiary	TPB
transferred intent	TI
unconscionable	uncon
unconstitutional	unconst
undue influence	u/e
Uniform Commercial Code	UCC
unilateral	uni
vendee	VE
vendor	VR
versus	v
void for vagueness	VFV
weight of authority	w/a
weight of the evidence	w/e
wife	W
with	w/
within	w/i
without	w/o
without prejudice	w/o/p
wrongful death	wr/d

Table of Cases

CHAPTER 1

What Is International Law?

Quick Reference Rules of Law

The Case of the S.S. "Lotus" (France v. Turkey)

Nation disputing jurisdiction (P) v. Nation disputing jurisdiction (D)

Permanent Ct. Int'l Justice, P.C.I.J., Ser. A, No. 10 (1927).

NATURE OF CASE: Action to determine validity of exercise of criminal jurisdiction.

FACT SUMMARY: France (P) contended that Turkey (D) violated international law by asserting jurisdiction over a French citizen who had been the first officer of a ship that collided with a Turkish ship on the high seas.

RULE OF LAW

There is no rule of international law prohibiting a State from exercising criminal jurisdiction over a foreign national who commits acts outside of the State's national jurisdiction.

FACTS: [Facts abbreviated in casebook excerpt.] A collision occurred between the French (P) mail steamer "Lotus," which was captained by Demons, a French citizen, and the Turkish (D) collier "Boz-Kourt," captained by Hassan Bey. When the "Lotus" arrived in Constantinople, Demons was placed under arrest. France (P) and Turkey (D) then agreed to submit to the Permanent Court of International Justice the question of whether the exercise of Turkish (D) criminal jurisdiction over Demons for an incident that occurred on the high seas violated international law.

ISSUE: Is there a rule of international law prohibiting a State from exercising criminal jurisdiction over a foreign national who commits acts outside of the State's national jurisdiction?

HOLDING AND DECISION: [Judge not stated in casebook excerpt.] No. There is no rule of international law prohibiting a State from exercising criminal jurisdiction over a foreign national who commits acts outside of the State's national jurisdiction. The first and foremost restriction imposed by international law upon a State is that, failing the existence of a permissive rule to the contrary, it may not exercise its power in any form in the territory of another State. It does not, however, follow that international law prohibits a State from exercising jurisdiction in its own territory, in respect of any case which relates to acts which have taken place abroad, and in which it cannot rely on some permissive rule of international law. The territoriality of criminal law is not an absolute principle of international law, and by no means coincides with territorial sovereignty. Here, because the effects of the alleged offense occurred on a Turkish (D) vessel, it is impossible to hold that there is a rule of international law which prohibits Turkey (D) from prosecuting Lieutenant Demons simply because he was aboard a French (P) ship at the time of the incident. Because there is no rule of international law in regard to collision cases to the effect that criminal proceedings are exclusively within the jurisdiction of the State whose flag is flown, both States here may exercise concurrent jurisdiction over this matter. Citation of a rule of international law authorizing a State to exercise jurisdiction in each case is not necessary.

ANALYSIS

In conformity with the holding of this case, France in 1975 enacted a law regarding its criminal jurisdiction over aliens. That law, cited in 102 *Journal Du Droit International* 962 (Clunet 1975), provides that aliens who commit a crime outside of the territory of the Republic may be prosecuted and judged pursuant to French law, when the victim is of French nationality. The holding in this case has been criticized by several eminent scholars for seeming to imply that international law permits all that it does not forbid.

Quicknotes

SOVEREIGNTY The absolute power conferred to the state to govern and regulate all persons located and activities conducted therein.

CHAPTER 2

The Creation of International Norms

Quick Reference Rules of Law

PAGE

1. **Termination and the Suspension of the Operations of Treaties.** (1) A fundamental change of circumstances must have been unforeseen and the existence of the circumstances at the time of the treaty's conclusion must have constituted an essential basis of the consent of the parties to be bound. (2) The doctrine of impossibility of performance may not be invoked for the termination of a treaty by a party to that treaty when it results from that party's own breach of an obligation flowing from the treaty. (Case Concerning the Gabcikovo-Nagymaros Project (Hungary v. Slovakia)) 4

Case Concerning the Gabcikovo-Nagymaros Project (Hungary v. Slovakia)

Treaty partner (D) v. Treaty partner (P)

Int'l. Ct. of Justice, I.C.J. 7 (1997).

NATURE OF CASE: Proceeding before the International Court of Justice.

FACT SUMMARY: Hungary claimed that changed circumstances made enforcement of a treaty with Slovakia impossible.

RULE OF LAW

(1) A fundamental change of circumstances must have been unforeseen and the existence of the circumstances at the time of the treaty's conclusion must have constituted an essential basis of the consent of the parties to be bound.
(2) The doctrine of impossibility of performance may not be invoked for the termination of a treaty by a party to that treaty when it results from that party's own breach of an obligation flowing from the treaty.

FACTS: Hungary (D) and Slovakia (P) had agreed in 1977 to build and operate a system of locks along the Danube River comprised of a dam, reservoir, hydroelectric power plant, and flood control improvements. This project was never completed and both countries underwent changes in their political and economic systems beginning in 1989. Hungary (D) first suspended and then abandoned its part of the works and later gave notice of termination of the treaty. In 1992, Hungary (D) and Slovakia (P) asked the I.C.J. to decide on the basis of international law whether Hungary (D) was entitled to suspend, and subsequently abandon, its part of the works, on the basis of the doctrine of impossibility of performance.

ISSUE:

(1) Must a fundamental change of circumstances have been unforeseen and must the existence of the circumstances at the time of the treaty's conclusion have constituted an essential basis of the consent of the parties to be bound?
(2) May the impossibility of performance doctrine be invoked for the termination of a treaty by a party to that treaty when it results from that party's own breach of an obligation flowing from the treaty?

HOLDING AND DECISION: [Judge not stated in casebook excerpt.]

(1) Yes. A fundamental change of circumstances must have been unforeseen and the existence of the circumstances at the time of the treaty's conclusion must have constituted an essential basis of the consent of the parties to be bound. Where the prevalent political and economic conditions were not so closely linked to the object and purpose of the treaty as to constitute an essential basis of the consent of the parties, there was no fundamental change of circumstances. The plea of fundamental change of circumstances may only be applied in exceptional cases.
(2) No. The doctrine of impossibility of performance may not be invoked for the termination of a treaty by a party to that treaty when it results from that party's own breach of an obligation flowing from the treaty. Hungary's (D) impossibility of performance argument fails, because if the joint exploitation of the investment was no longer possible, it was originally because Hungary (D) did not carry out its side of the deal.

ANALYSIS

The court relied on the Vienna Convention, even though the parties had not ratified the Vienna Convention at the time of their treaty. The Vienna Convention may be seen as a codification of existing customary law on the subject of termination of a treaty on the basis of change in circumstances. New developments in environmental law were not completely unforeseen.

Quicknotes

DOCTRINE OF IMPOSSIBILITY A doctrine relieving the parties to a contract from liability for nonperformance of their duties thereunder, if the subject matter of the contract ceases to exist, a person essential to the performance of the contract is deceased, or the service or goods contracted for have become illegal.

ENVIRONMENTAL LAW A body of federal law passed in 1970 which protects the environment against public and private actions that harm the ecosystem.

TREATY An agreement between two or more nations for the benefit of the general public.

CHAPTER 3

International Law in the United States

Quick Reference Rules of Law

CHAPTER 3

Missouri v. Holland

State (P) v. Game warden (D)

252 U.S. 416 (1920).

NATURE OF CASE: State appeal of action seeking a declaratory judgment.

FACT SUMMARY: Missouri (P) brought this suit to prevent Holland (D), a game warden of the United States, from attempting to enforce the Migratory Bird Treaty Act on the ground that the statute was an unconstitutional interference with the rights reserved to the states by the Tenth Amendment.

RULE OF LAW

Acts of Congress are the supreme law of the land only when made in pursuance of the Constitution, while treaties are declared to be so when made under the authority of the United States.

FACTS: The state of Missouri (P) brought this bill in equity to prevent Holland (D), a game warden of the United States, from attempting to enforce the Migratory Bird Treaty Act, the enactment statute of a treaty between the United States and Great Britain, proclaimed by the President and intended to protect the birds. The bill charges that the statute is an unconstitutional interference with the rights reserved to the states by the Tenth Amendment, and that the acts of Holland (D) done and threatened under that authority invade the sovereign right of the state of Missouri (P) and contravene its will manifested in statutes. A motion to dismiss was sustained by the district court on the ground that the act of Congress is constitutional.

ISSUE: Are treaties the supreme law of the land when made under the authority of the United States?

HOLDING AND DECISION: (Holmes, J.) Yes. Treaties are the supreme law of the land when made under the authority of the United States. While it is true that acts of Congress are the supreme law of the land only when made in pursuance of the Constitution, treaties are declared to be so when made under the authority of the United States. Furthermore, valid treaties are as binding within the territorial limits of the states as they are elsewhere throughout the dominion of the United States. Since the Migratory Bird Treaty Act was made pursuant to a treaty between the United States and Great Britain, its provisions are the supreme law of the land and binding on the state of Missouri. The treaty and the statute must be upheld. The decree of the lower court is affirmed.

ANALYSIS

Justice Sutherland, in discussing the foreign affairs power in *United States v. Curtiss-Wright Export Corp.*, 299 U.S. 304 (1936), stated that as a result of the separation from Great Britain by the colonies acting as a unit, the powers of external sovereignty passed from the Crown not to the colonies severally, but to the colonies in their collective and corporate capacity as the United States. Even before the Declaration, the colonies were a unit in foreign affairs, and the powers to make treaties and maintain diplomatic relations, if they had never been mentioned in the Constitution, would have vested in the federal government as necessary concomitants of nationality.

Quicknotes

DECLARATORY JUDGMENT An adjudication by the courts which grants not relief but is binding over the legal status of the parties involved in the dispute.

EQUITY Fairness; justice; the determination of a matter consistent with principles of fairness and not in strict compliance with rules of law.

JURISDICTION The authority of a court to hear and declare judgment in respect to a particular matter.

TENTH AMENDMENT The Tenth Amendment to the United States Constitution reserving those powers therein, not expressly delegated to the federal government or prohibited to the states or to the people.

TREATY An agreement between two or more nations for the benefit of the general public.

Reid v. Covert

[Parties not identified.]

354 U.S. 1 (1957).

NATURE OF CASE: Appeal from a writ of habeas corpus.

FACT SUMMARY: [Facts were abbreviated in casebook excerpt.] Civilian spouses of soldiers who murdered their husbands were tried by court-martial under the Uniform Code of Military Justice, without grand jury or jury trial, and they were sentenced to death.

RULE OF LAW

Civilian dependents accompanying soldiers on active duty overseas could not constitutionally be subjected to military court-martial for offenses committed overseas, despite treaties or executive branch agreements to the contrary.

FACTS: [Facts were abbreviated in casebook excerpt.] Certain civilian spouses murdered their husbands on the foreign bases where they were stationed. They were tried by court-martial under the Uniform Code of Military Justice, which permitted the trials without grand jury or jury trial, and they were sentenced to death.

ISSUE: Can civilian dependents accompanying soldiers on active duty overseas constitutionally be subjected to military court-martial for offenses committed overseas?

HOLDING AND DECISION: (Black, J.) No. Civilian dependents accompanying soldiers on active duty overseas cannot constitutionally be subjected to military court-martial for offenses committed overseas. No agreement with a foreign nation can confer power on Congress, or on any other branch of government, that is free from the restraints of the Constitution. There is nothing in the language of the Supremacy Clause that intimates that the treaties and laws enacted pursuant to them do not have to comply with the provisions of the Constitution. Military trials for civilian dependents, accompanying soldiers on active duty overseas, would deprive them of the protections of Section 2 of Article II and the Fifth and Sixth Amendments, which require that crimes be tried by a jury after indictment by a grand jury. Since the court-martial of Mrs. Covert did not meet these requirements, it was not constitutionally permitted. There is no indication that the founders contemplated setting up a rival system of military courts to compete with civilian courts for jurisdiction over civilians who might have some contact or relationship with the armed forces.

CONCURRENCE: (Harlan, J.) The sweeping proposition that a full Article III trial may not be required in every case for the trial of a civilian dependent of a serviceman overseas. There are provisions of the Constitution that do not necessarily apply in all circumstances in every foreign place. The big question is which constitutional guarantees should apply to a particular set of circumstances.

ANALYSIS

The Supreme Court stated in this opinion that the idea that the relatives of soldiers could be denied a jury trial in a court of law and instead be tried by court-martial under the guise of regulating the armed forces would have seemed incredible to the Founding Fathers, in whose lifetime the right of the military to try soldiers for any offenses in time of peace had only been grudgingly conceded.

Quicknotes

EXECUTIVE AGREEMENT An agreement with a foreign nation that is binding on the country, entered into by the President without Senate approval.

SUPREMACY CLAUSE Article VI, Sec. 2, of the Constitution, which provides that federal action must prevail over inconsistent state action.

TREATY An agreement between two or more nations for the benefit of the general public.

WRIT OF HABEAS CORPUS A proceeding in which a defendant brings a writ to compel a judicial determination of whether he is lawfully being held in custody.

Asakura v. City of Seattle

Japanese national (P) v. City (D)

265 U.S. 332 (1924).

NATURE OF CASE: Appeal from an action seeking an injunction of a city ordinance.

FACT SUMMARY: Asakura (P), a Japanese national residing in Seattle and engaged in business there as a pawnbroker, brought this suit against the City of Seattle (D) attacking the validity of a city ordinance denying a license to engage in pawnbroking to anyone not a citizen of the United States and seeking an injunction against its enforcement.

RULE OF LAW

Pursuant to Article VI of the Constitution, a treaty made under the authority of the United States shall be the supreme law of the land, and the judges in every state shall be bound thereby, anything in the constitution or laws of any state to the contrary notwithstanding.

FACTS: Asakura (P), a Japanese national residing in Seattle and engaged in business there as a pawnbroker, brought this suit attacking the validity of an ordinance of the city of Seattle (D). The ordinance makes it unlawful for any person to engage in the business of pawnbroking unless he shall have a license, and no such license shall be granted unless the applicant is a citizen of the United States. Asakura (P) seeks an injunction against enforcement of the ordinance and attacks its validity on the on the ground that it violates the treaty between the United States and Japan of 1911. The treaty provides in part that the citizens of the contracting parties shall be free to carry on trade, to lease land for residential and commercial purposes, and to do anything incident to or necessary for trade in the territories of the other upon the same terms as native citizens. The Supreme Court of Washington reversed a decision below in favor of Asakura (P), and he appealed.

ISSUE: Is a treaty made under the authority of the United States, the supreme law of the land, contrary state laws notwithstanding?

HOLDING AND DECISION: (Butler, J.) Yes. Article VI of the Constitution makes a treaty under the authority of the United States the supreme law of the land. The treaty-making power of the United States is not limited by any express provision of the Constitution, and, though it does not extend so far as to authorize what the Constitution forbids, it does extend to all proper subjects of negotiation between our government and other nations. The treaty between the United States and Japan establishes the rule of equality between Japanese subjects while in this country and native citizens. The treaty is binding within the state of Washington. The rule of equality established by it cannot be rendered nugatory in any part of the United States by municipal ordinance or state laws. The treaty stands on the same footing of supremacy, as do the provisions of the Constitution and laws of the United States. The business of pawnbroking is trade within the meaning of the treaty and the ordinance violates it by making it impossible for aliens to carry on that business. The decree of the Supreme Court of Washington is therefore reversed.

ANALYSIS

The treaty involved in the case at bar operated without the aid of any legislation, state, or national, and it will be applied and given authoritative effect by the courts. It was a self-executing treaty. Other treaties cannot be enforced without enacting legislation by Congress. These treaties, without an enabling statute passed by Congress, cannot become a rule for the courts.

Quicknotes

INJUNCTION A court order requiring a person to do or prohibiting that person from doing a specific act.

TREATY An agreement between two or more nations for the benefit of the general public.

Medellín v. Texas

Mexican national (D) v. State (P)

552 U.S. 491 (2008).

NATURE OF CASE: Appeal of death sentence.

FACT SUMMARY: After Texas (P) convicted José Medellín (D), he appealed on the grounds that Texas (P) failed to inform him of his right to have consular personnel notified of his detention by the state, as required under the Vienna Convention. On appeal to the United States Supreme Court, Medellín (D) argued that a case decided by the International Court of Justice suggested that his conviction must be reconsidered to comply with the Vienna Convention.

RULE OF LAW

(1) The U.S. Constitution does not require state courts to honor a treaty obligation of the United States by enforcing a decision of the International Court of Justice.

(2) The President does not have the constitutional authority to unilaterally convert a non-self-executing treaty into a self-executing one that applies domestically to the United States.

FACTS: José Medellín (D), a Mexican national, was convicted and sentenced. In his appeal, Medellín (D) argued that the state had violated his rights under the Vienna Convention, to which the United States is a party. Article 36 of the Vienna Convention gives any foreign national detained for a crime the right to contact his consulate. The United States Supreme Court dismissed the petition and Medellín's (D) case was remanded to the Texas Court of Criminal Appeals, which also denied him relief. The United States Supreme Court took up his case again, and Medellín's (D) argument rested in part on a holding by the International Court of Justice (ICJ) in *Case Concerning Avena and Other Mexican Nationals (Mex. v. U.S.)*, 2004 I.C.J. 12, that the United States had violated the Vienna Convention rights of 51 Mexican nationals (including Medellín (D)) and that their state-court convictions must be reconsidered, regardless of any forfeiture of the right to raise the Vienna Convention claims because of a failure to follow state rules governing criminal convictions. Medellín (D) argued that the Vienna Convention granted him an individual right that state courts must respect. Medellín (D) also cited a memorandum from the U.S. President that instructed state courts to comply with the ICJ's rulings by rehearing the cases. Medellín (D) argued that the Constitution gives the President broad power to ensure that treaties are enforced, and that this power extends to the treatment of treaties in state court proceedings.

ISSUE:

(1) Does the U.S. Constitution require state courts to honor a treaty obligation of the United States by enforcing a decision of the International Court of Justice?

(2) Does the President have the constitutional authority to unilaterally convert a non-self-executing treaty into a self-executing one that applies domestically to the United States?

HOLDING AND DECISION: (Roberts, C.J.)

(1) No. The U.S. Constitution does not require state courts to honor a treaty obligation of the United States by enforcing a decision of the International Court of Justice. The Vienna Convention provides that if a person detained by a foreign country asks, the authorities of the detaining national must, without delay, inform the consular post of the detainee of the detention. The Optional Protocol of the Convention provides that the International Court of Justice is the venue for resolution of issues of interpretation of the Vienna Convention. By ratifying the Optional Protocol to the Vienna Convention, the United States consented to the jurisdiction of the ICJ with respect to claims arising out of the Vienna Convention. In 2005, however, after *Avena* was decided, the United States gave notice of withdrawal from the Optional Protocol. While *Avena* constitutes an international law obligation on the part of the United States, it does not help Medellín (D) because not all international law obligations automatically constitute binding federal law. *Avena* does not have automatic domestic legal effect in state and federal courts. There are two ways an international treaty may become legally binding in the United States. First, it can be a self-executing treaty containing express language regarding its binging effect domestically. Second, Congress can enact legislation implementing the treaty if the treaty itself does not contain the self-executing language. Here, neither scenario occurred. Thus, the ICJ judgment is not automatically enforceable domestic law, immediately and directly binding on state and federal courts under the Supremacy Clause.

(2) No. The President does not have the constitutional authority to unilaterally convert a non-self-executing treaty into a self-executing one that applies domestically in the United States. The Presidential Memorandum was an attempt by the executive branch to enforce a non-self-executing treaty without the necessary

Continued on next page.

congressional action. The constitutional authority for such action lies only with Congress. Judgment affirmed.

CONCURRENCE: (Stevens, J.) Although the judgment is correct, Texas (P) ought to comply with *Avena. Avena* may not be the supreme law of the land, but it constitutes an international law obligation on the part of the United States. Since Texas (P) failed to provide consular notice in accordance with the Vienna Convention, thereby getting the United States into this mess, and since that violation probably didn't prejudice Medellín (D), Texas (P) ought to comply with *Avena.*

DISSENT: (Breyer, J.) The majority does not point to a single ratified U.S. treaty that contains the self-executing language it says is required in this case. The absence or presence of language in a treaty about a provision's self-execution proves nothing. The relevant treaty provisions should be found to be self-executing, because (1) the language supports direct judicial enforceability, (2) the Optional Protocol applies to disputes about the meaning of a provision that is itself self-executing and judicially enforceable, (3) logic requires a conclusion that the provision is self-executing since it is "final" and "binding," (4) the majority's decision has negative practical implications, (5) the ICJ judgment is well suited to direct judicial enforcement, (6) such a holding would not threaten constitutional conflict with other branches, and (7) neither the President nor Congress has expressed concern about direct judicial enforcement of the ICJ decision.

ANALYSIS

Medellín (D) was executed on August 5, 2008, after last-minute appeals to the United States Supreme Court were rejected. Governor Rick Perry rejected calls from Mexico and Secretary of State Condoleezza Rice and Attorney General Michael Mukasey to delay the execution, citing the torture, rape, and strangulation of two teenage girls in Houston as just cause for the death penalty. Though a bill was introduced in the House of Representatives to respond to the Court's ruling, Congress took no action.

Breard v. Greene

Convicted murderer (D) v. State (P)

523 U.S. 371 (1998).

NATURE OF CASE: Appeal from denial of habeas corpus.

FACT SUMMARY: Breard (P) claimed that his conviction should be overturned because of alleged violations of the Vienna Convention on Consular Relations.

RULE OF LAW

When a statute which is subsequent in time is inconsistent with a treaty, the statute to the extent of conflict renders the treaty null.

FACTS: Breard (P) was scheduled to be executed following his conviction for murder. Breard (P) filed for habeas relief in federal court, arguing that the arresting authorities had wrongfully failed to inform him that, as a foreign national, he had the right to contact the Paraguayan consulate (P). The claim was rejected by the district court and the court of appeals affirmed, because he failed to raise it in state court, as required by U.S. law. Five years later, the Republic of Paraguay instituted proceedings against the United States in the International Court of Justice (ICJ), charging that the United States violated the Vienna Convention when Breard was arrested. The ICJ stayed the execution until the final decision. Breard (P) then filed a petition for an original writ of habeas corpus and a stay application in the United States Supreme Court to enforce the ICJ's order.

ISSUE: When a statute that is subsequent in time is inconsistent with a treaty, does the statute render the treaty null?

HOLDING AND DECISION: (Per curiam) Yes. When a statute that is subsequent in time is inconsistent with a treaty, the statute to the extent of conflict renders the treaty null. Breard's (P) argument that the Vienna Convention was violated must fail because Congress enacted the Antiterrorism and Effective Death Penalty Act after the Vienna Convention, which provides that a habeas petitioner alleging that he is held in violation of a treaty of the United States will not, as a general rule, be afforded an evidentiary hearing if he has failed to develop the factual basis of the claim in state court. The executive branch has authority over foreign relations and may utilize diplomatic channels to request a stay of execution. Petition denied.

ANALYSIS

Though not explained in the casebook excerpt, the Court also held that the Eleventh Amendment barred suits against states. The Consul General of Paraguay tried to raise a § 1983 suit. The Court found that Paraguay was not authorized to do so.

Quicknotes

42 U.S.C. § 1983 Provides that every person, who under color of state law subjects or causes to be subjected any citizen of the United States or person within its jurisdiction to be deprived of rights, privileges and immunities guaranteed by the federal Constitution and laws, is liable to the injured party at law or in equity.

ELEVENTH AMENDMENT The Eleventh Amendment to the United States Constitution prohibiting the extension of the judicial powers of the federal courts to suits brought against a state by citizens of another state, or of a foreign state, without the state's consent.

HABEAS CORPUS A proceeding in which a defendant brings a writ to compel a judicial determination of whether he is lawfully being held in custody.

United States v. Curtiss-Wright Corp.

Federal government (P) v. Arms dealer (D)

299 U.S. 304 (1936).

NATURE OF CASE: Appeal from indictment for conspiracy to sell arms of war.

FACT SUMMARY: Curtiss-Wright Corp. (D) sold 15 machine guns to Bolivia, a country engaged in armed conflict in the Chaco, in violation of a joint resolution of Congress and a presidential proclamation.

RULE OF LAW

Congress may grant the President freedom to issue proclamations outlawing domestic actions that frustrate or obstruct his conduct of foreign affairs.

FACTS: By joint resolution in 1934, Congress authorized the President to issue a proclamation prohibiting within the United States the sale of arms to countries involved in armed conflict in the Chaco. On the same day the resolution was adopted, President Roosevelt issued such a proclamation. In 1936 Curtiss-Wright Corp. (D) was indicted for conspiring to sell within the United States 15 machine guns to Bolivia, one of the countries engaged in war in the Chaco. Curtiss-Wright (D) appealed the indictment on the grounds that Congress, in its adoption of the joint resolution, had unconstitutionally delegated its legislative power over internal affairs to the executive branch.

ISSUE: May Congress grant the President authority to issue proclamations outlawing domestic actions that frustrate or obstruct his conduct of foreign policy?

HOLDING AND DECISION: (Sutherland, J.) Yes. Congress may grant the President freedom to issue proclamations outlawing domestic actions that frustrate or obstruct his conduct of foreign affairs. The President is the sole organ of the federal government in the field of international relations; his powers in this area are limited only by the Constitution itself. His authority in the foreign arena was settled at the time the American colonies declared their independence from Great Britain; the powers to conduct foreign and external affairs, which had heretofore been vested exclusively in the British Crown, then passed directly to the colonies in their collective and corporate capacity as the United States. These powers, to declare and wage war, to conclude peace, to make treaties, to maintain diplomatic relations with other sovereignties, vest in the President and the federal government as a necessary concomitant of nationality itself. Congressional power over internal affairs, on the other hand, was based on specific enumeration and "necessary and proper" implied powers, and derived from power over domestic matters which the colonies had heretofore possessed severally and exercised individually. Thus, congressional legislation, such as the joint resolution here, which is made effective through negotiation and inquiry in the international field must often accord to the President a degree of discretion and freedom from statutory restriction which would not be admissible were domestic affairs alone involved. The President, not Congress, has the better opportunity of knowing the conditions which prevail in foreign countries; he has his agents and confidential sources. Therefore, the joint resolution was constitutional and not an improper delegation of power to the executive branch. Affirmed.

ANALYSIS

Justice Sutherland also noted other "powers" in foreign affairs which were "inherently inseparable" from the concept of nationality. These included the powers to acquire territory by discovery and occupation, to expel undesirable aliens, and to make international agreements which are not treaties as defined by the Constitution. It must be noted, however, that the joint resolution at issue here did not expressly allow the President to make the sale of arms to belligerents in the Chaco a criminal act, and Curtiss-Wright (D) was indicted for criminal conspiracy. However, Justice Sutherland implicitly found that President Roosevelt's construction of the resolution as allowing him the power to criminally prosecute sellers of arms of war was reasonable.

Quicknotes

ENUMERATED POWERS Specific powers mentioned in, and granted by, the Constitution, e.g., the taxing power.

IMPLIED POWERS Powers impliedly delegated to the various branches of government that, while not expressly stated in the Constitution, are necessary to effectuate the enumerated powers.

Youngstown Sheet & Tube Co. v. Sawyer

Steel manufacturers (P) v. Federal government (D)

343 U.S. 579 (1952).

NATURE OF CASE: Suit for declaratory and injunctive relief from a presidential order.

FACT SUMMARY: Faced with an imminent steel strike during the Korean War, the President ordered governmental seizure of the steel companies to prevent the strike. The companies challenged his power to take such action as being without constitutional authority or prior congressional approval.

RULE OF LAW

The President, as leader of the executive branch, is bound to enforce the laws within the limits of the authority expressly granted to him by the Constitution, and he cannot usurp the lawmaking power of Congress by an assertion of an unspecified aggregation of his specified powers.

FACTS: As a result of long, but unsuccessful, negotiations with various steel companies, the United Steelworkers of America served notice of intent to strike in April 1952. Through the last months of the negotiating the President had utilized every available administrative remedy to effect a settlement and avert a strike. Congress had engaged in extensive debate on solutions but had passed no legislation on the issue. By order of the President, the Secretary of Commerce seized the steel companies so that steel production would not be interrupted during the Korean War. The steel companies sued in federal district court to have the seizure order declared invalid and to enjoin its enforcement. The government asserted that the President had "inherent power" to make the order and that it was "supported by the Constitution, historical precedent and court decisions." The district court granted a preliminary injunction which was stayed the same day by the court of appeals. The United States Supreme Court granted certiorari and ordered immediate argument.

ISSUE: May the President, relying on a concept of inherent powers, and in his capacity as Commander in Chief, make an order which usurps the lawmaking authority of Congress on the basis of a compelling need to protect the national security?

HOLDING AND DECISION: (Black, J.) No. The President cannot usurp the lawmaking power of Congress by an assertion of an unspecified aggregation of his specified powers. In the absence of express authority for the President's act, it is argued that the power can be implied from the aggregate of his express powers granted by the Constitution. This order cannot be justified by reliance on the President's role as Commander in Chief. Even though the term "theater of war" has enjoyed an expanding definition, it cannot embrace the taking of private property to prevent a strike. The President's powers in the area of legislation are limited to proposing new laws to the Congress or vetoing laws which he deems inadvisable. This order is not executive implementation of a congressional act but a legislative act performed by the President. Only Congress may do what the President has attempted here. The Constitution is specific in vesting the lawmaking powers in Congress and we, therefore, affirm the district court's decision to enjoin the enforcement of this order.

CONCURRENCE: (Jackson, J.) Presidential power is most vast where there is either express or implied authorization of Congress, less vast where Congress has not granted or denied authority, and most limited when Congress expressly or impliedly denies him power. The executive seizure of the steel industry in this case is justified only by the severe tests under the third grouping. It can be supported only of it is within his domain and beyond control by Congress. But the seizure is legislative in nature, and is therefore not beyond the control of Congress. And the President does not have legislative power, except to recommend and veto. The seizure cannot be justified by his power as Commander in Chief of the armed forces, or from any number of inherent powers never expressly granted by said to have accrued to the office from historical practice. Since the seizure is legislative in character, it falls within congressional power.

ANALYSIS

Justice Black's broad language was criticized by many scholars as being overly expansive for the case presented. However, other authorities pointed out that the broad arguments advanced by the government required a broad response. During oral argument before the Court, the government counsel stated that while the Constitution imposed limits on congressional and judicial powers, no such limits were imposed on the presidency. While supplemental briefs were filed modifying this position, the damage may already have been done. The Court was faced with a paucity of judicial precedents. The President and Congress have traditionally preferred political rather than judicial solutions to their conflicts. This practice avoids the limitations imposed on future actions by binding judicial precedents. Furthermore, as can be seen by the cases of *Marbury v. Madison*, 5 U.S. 137 (1803) and *United States v. Nixon*, 418 U.S. 683 (1974), the executive branch

Continued on next page.

has not fared well when it has submitted to judicial jurisdiction.

Quicknotes

VETO A refusal by the President or a governor to sign into law a bill that has been passed by a legislature.

United States v. Pink

Federal government (P) v. State (D)

315 U.S. 203 (1942).

NATURE OF CASE: Appeal from an action to recover the assets of a foreign company.

FACT SUMMARY: Pursuant to the Litvinov Assignment, the United States (P), assignee of the Soviet Union, sued Pink (D), the New York Superintendent of Insurance, who had succeeded to the assets of the New York branch of a Russian insurance company previously nationalized by Soviet law.

RULE OF LAW
State law must yield when it is inconsistent with, or impairs the policy or provisions of, a treaty or an international compact or agreement.

FACTS: As an incident to U.S. recognition of the U.S.S.R., Litvinov, the Soviet foreign minister, delivered a letter to the President of the United States (P) by which the Soviet Union assigned to the United States (P) amounts due to the Soviet Union from United States nationals. The United States (P) as assignee of the Soviet Union sued Pink (D), the New York Superintendent of Insurance, who had succeeded by a court order to the assets of the New York branch of a Russian insurance company previously nationalized by Soviet law. The New York courts had dismissed the United States' (P) complaint on the ground that the Russian nationalization decrees were extraterritorial, confiscatory, and contrary to the public policy of New York. The United States (P) appealed to the United States Supreme Court.

ISSUE: Must state law yield when it is inconsistent with, or impairs the policy or provisions of, a treaty or an international compact or agreement?

HOLDING AND DECISION: (Dougias, J.) Yes. The powers of the President in the conduct of foreign relations included the power, without consent of the Senate, to determine the public policy of the United States with respect to the Russian nationalization decrees. This court has recognized that the Litvinov Assignment was an international compact which did not require the participation of the Senate. It is, of course, true that even treaties with foreign nations will be carefully construed so as not to derogate from the authority and jurisdiction of the states of this nation unless clearly necessary to effectuate the national policy. But state law must yield when it is inconsistent with, or impairs the policy or provisions of, a treaty or of an international compact or agreement. Thus, the power of a state to refuse enforcement of rights based on foreign law that runs counter to the public policy of the forum must give way before the superior federal policy evidenced by a treaty or international compact or agreement. In the case at bar, enforcement of New York's policy could collide with the federal policy. The decision of the state court is reversed.

ANALYSIS

The power to remove obstacles to full recognition of a foreign government such as settlement of the claims of their nationals is an implied power of the President who is the sole organ of the federal government in the field of international relations. In the instant case it was the judgment of the political department that recognition of the Soviet Union and the Litvinov Assignment were interdependent.

Quicknotes

IMPLIED POWERS Powers impliedly delegated to the various branches of government that, while not expressly stated in the Constitution, are necessary to effectuate the enumerated powers.

TREATY An agreement between two or more nations for the benefit of the general public.

Dames & Moore v. Regan

Claimant (P) v. Federal government (D)

453 U.S. 654 (1981).

NATURE OF CASE: Review of challenge to executive order nullifying certain judgments against Iran.

FACT SUMMARY: The President, in settlement of the Iran hostage crisis, executed an order nullifying certain judgments against Iran.

RULE OF LAW

The President may issue an order nullifying judgments against a foreign state.

FACTS: Dames & Moore (P) obtained a favorable judgment in a breach of contract action against the Iranian government. Around the same time, the United States and Iran entered into a resolution of the hostage crisis. Part of this settlement called for arbitration of disputes between U.S. nationals and the Iranian government. Pursuant to this, President Carter issued an executive order invalidating all unexecuted judgments against Iran and releasing all attachments and garnishments. Dames & Moore (P) challenged the validity of this order. The district court upheld the order, and the United States Supreme Court granted expedited review.

ISSUE: May the President issue an order nullifying judgments against a foreign state?

HOLDING AND DECISION: (Rehnquist, J.) Yes. The President may issue an order nullifying judgments against a foreign state. The International Emergency Economic Powers Act (IEEPA) constitutes specific congressional authorization to the President to nullify the attachments and order the transfer of Iranian assets. But the IEEPA does not authorize the suspension of claims pending in American courts of American citizens against Iran. Nor does the Hostage Act constitute specific authorization of the President to suspend claims in American courts. But Congress has acquiesced in a long-standing practice of claims settlement by executive agreement. Both IEEPA and the Hostage Act grant broad powers to the President, and while they do not specifically grant the President power to settle the claims in this case, they are nevertheless highly relevant because they indicate congressional acceptance of a broad scope for executive action in these circumstances. In addition, Congress has historically implicitly approved the practice of claim settlement by executive agreement, by enacting and frequently amending the International Claims Settlement Act. And, finally, the legislative history of the IEEPA reveals that Congress has accepted the authority of the executive branch to enter into settlement agreements. Affirmed.

ANALYSIS

Whenever presidential power is analyzed, the chief authority is usually *Youngstown Sheet & Tube Co. v. Sawyer*, 343 U.S. 579 (1952). Justice Jackson's concurrence is the most oft-quoted portion of the opinion. The concept of presidential power encompassing a spectrum from congressional authorization to congressional opposition was most clearly articulated there.

Quicknotes

ARBITRATION An agreement to have a dispute heard and decided by a neutral third party, rather than through legal proceedings.

EXECUTIVE ORDER An order issued by the President, or another executive of government, which has the force of law.

Hamdi v. Rumsfeld

Suspected terrorist (P) v. United States (D)

542 U.S. 507 (2004).

NATURE OF CASE: Unlawful detention claim.

FACT SUMMARY: Hamdi (P), who fought for the Taliban, claimed he was unlawfully detained by the U.S. government (D).

RULE OF LAW

The executive branch of the U.S. government is authorized to deter citizens who it suspects were part of or supporting forces hostile to the United States or coalition partners in Afghanistan and who engaged in armed conflict against the United States there.

FACTS: Hamdi (P), who fought for the Taliban, claimed he was unlawfully detained by the U.S. government (D). His father brought a habeas corpus petition, and the Department of Defense sent a declaration alleging details of Hamdi's (P) associations with the Taliban. The district court found the declaration alone did not support Hamdi's (P) detention and ordered the government (D) to provide other materials of a sensitive nature for in camera review. The Fourth Circuit ordered the habeas petition dismissed, reversing the district court's order. The appeals court held that because Hamdi (P) was captured in an active combat zone, no factual inquiry was necessary.

ISSUE: Is the executive branch of the U.S. government authorized to deter citizens who it suspects were part of or supporting forces hostile to the United States or coalition partners in Afghanistan and who engaged in armed conflict against the United States there?

HOLDING AND DECISION: (O'Connor, J.) Yes. The executive branch of the U.S. government is authorized to deter citizens who it suspects were part of or supporting forces hostile to the United States or coalition partners in Afghanistan and who engaged in armed conflict against the United States there. Congress's Authorization for the Use of Military Force (AUMF) authorizes the President to use necessary force against nations associated with the terrorist attacks on September 11, 2001, and individuals who fought as part of the Taliban are individuals Congress sought to target in passing the AUMF. In addition, detention of lawful and unlawful combatants is an incident of war that is acceptable, though the law of war requires that detention may last no longer than active hostilities. The judgment of the Fourth Circuit is vacated and the case is remanded.

CONCURRENCE AND DISSENT: (Souter, J.) The plurality is correct in its conclusion that Hamdi (P) had the right to challenge in court his status as an enemy combatant, but is incorrect in concluding that Congress authorized Hamdi's (P) detention through the Force Resolution.

DISSENT: (Scalia, J.) Only a suspension of the writ of habeas corpus, which had not occurred, could justify Hamdi's (P) detention without charges being brought.

DISSENT: (Thomas, J.) The detention of Hamdi (P) as an enemy combatant, and the President's determination that he should be detained, falls within the federal government's war powers, and the court should not second-guess the decision. The President may have inherent power to make that decision, but the question need not be addressed, since the AUMF authorized the President to do so.

ANALYSIS

The U.S. government has claimed that no Taliban detainee is entitled to prisoner of war status. This would appear to be in violation of the Geneva Convention, which provides that where a prisoner's status is undetermined, the prisoner is entitled to "prisoner of war" status.

Quicknotes

GENEVA CONVENTION International agreement that governs the conduct of warring nations.

Hamdan v. Rumsfeld

Detained terrorist (P) v. United States (D)

548 U.S. 557 (2006).

NATURE OF CASE: Appeal from circuit court holding that a military commission violated a detainee's rights under the Geneva Convention.

FACT SUMMARY: A U.S. military commission began proceedings against Hamdan (P), who was captured in Afghanistan. Hamdan (P) challenged the authority of the commission.

RULE OF LAW

(1) The military commission established to try those deemed "enemy combatants" for alleged war crimes in the War on Terror was not authorized by the Congress or the inherent powers of the President.
(2) The rights protected by the Geneva Convention may be enforced in federal court through habeas corpus petitions.

FACTS: Salim Ahmed Hamdan (P) was captured by Afghani forces and imprisoned by the U.S. military in Guantanamo Bay. He filed a petition for a writ of habeas corpus in federal district court to challenge his detention. Before the district court ruled on the petition, a U.S. military commission began proceedings against Hamdan (P), which designated him an enemy combatant. Hamdan (P) challenged the authority of the commission, arguing that the commission trial would violate his rights under Article 102 of the Geneva Convention, which provides that a "prisoner of war can be validly sentenced only if the sentence has been pronounced by the same courts according to the same procedure as in the case of members of the armed forces of the Detaining Power." The district court granted Hamdan's (P) habeas petition, ruling that a hearing to determine whether he was a prisoner of war under the Geneva Convention must have taken place before he could be tried by a military commission. The D.C. Circuit Court of Appeals reversed the decision, finding that the Geneva Convention could not be enforced in federal court and that the establishment of military tribunals had been authorized by Congress and was therefore not unconstitutional.

ISSUE:

(1) Was the military commission established to try those deemed "enemy combatants" for alleged war crimes in the War on Terror authorized by the Congress or the inherent powers of the President?
(2) May the rights protected by the Geneva Convention be enforced in federal court through habeas corpus petitions?

HOLDING AND DECISION: (Stevens, J.)

(1) No. The military commission established to try those deemed "enemy combatants" for alleged war crimes in the War on Terror was not authorized by the Congress or the inherent powers of the President. Neither an act of Congress nor the inherent powers of the executive branch laid out in the Constitution expressly authorized the sort of military commission at issue in this case. Absent that express authorization, the commission had to comply with the ordinary laws of the United States and the laws of war.
(2) Yes. The rights protected by the Geneva Convention may be enforced in federal court through habeas corpus petitions. The Geneva Convention, as a part of the ordinary laws of war, could be enforced by the Supreme Court, along with the statutory Uniform Code of Military Justice (UCMJ), since the military commission was not authorized. Hamdan's (P) exclusion from certain parts of his trial deemed classified by the military commission violated both of these, and the trial was therefore illegal. Judgment reversed and case remanded.

CONCURRENCE: (Breyer, J.) Congress has denied the President the legislative authority to create military commissions of the kind at issue here, but nothing prevents him from seeking such authority he believes necessary.

CONCURRENCE: (Kennedy, J.) Congress set forth governing principles for military courts in the UCMJ, which limits the President's authority to establish commissions such as the one in this case. It also contravenes the law of war, in that the commission was not a regularly constituted court affording judicial guarantees for the individual on trial.

DISSENT: (Thomas, J.) The President's decision to establish the commission is entitled to deference. Under the Authorization for the Use of Military Force (AUMF), Congress authorized the President to use all necessary force against those persons he determines planned or aided the attacks. The majority was incorrect in failing to apply the AUMF to this case.

DISSENT: (Alito, J.) The military commission satisfied the UCMJ's requirement that it be a regularly constituted court. Compliance with the procedures of the UCMJ was not required for a regularly constituted court, and the military commission's procedures were adequate to guarantee against summary justice.

Continued on next page.

ANALYSIS

Many U.S. and international human rights organizations have determined that violations might occur through the non-application of the Geneva Convention to detainees in the U.S. war on terrorism.

Quicknotes

GENEVA CONVENTION International agreement that governs the conduct of warring nations.

The Paquete Habana

Ship owners (P) v. Ship owners (D)

175 U.S. 677 (1900).

NATURE OF CASE: Appeal from judgment condemning two fishing vessels and their cargoes as prizes of war.

FACT SUMMARY: The owners of fishing vessels seized by officials of the United States argued that international law exempted coastal fishermen from capture as prizes of war.

RULE OF LAW
Coastal fishing vessels, with their cargoes and crews, are exempt from capture as prizes of war.

FACTS: The owners of two separate fishing vessels brought this appeal of a district court decree condemning two fishing vessels and their cargoes as prizes of war. Each vessel was a fishing smack, running in and out of Havana, sailing under the Spanish flag, and regularly engaged in fishing on the coast of Cuba. The cargoes of both vessels consisted of fresh fish, which had been caught by their respective crews. Until stopped by the blockading United States squadron, the owners had no knowledge of the existence of a war or of any blockage. The owners had no arms or ammunition on board the vessels and had made no attempt to run the blockade after learning of its existence. The owners did not offer any resistance at the time of capture. On appeal, the owners argued that both customary international law and the writings of leading international scholars recognized an exemption from seizure at wartime of coastal fishing vessels.

ISSUE: Are coastal fishing vessels, with their cargoes and crews, exempt from capture as prizes of war?

HOLDING AND DECISION: (Gray, J.) Yes. Coastal fishing vessels, pursuing their vocation of catching and bringing in fresh fish, have been recognized as exempt, with their cargoes and crews, from capture as prizes of war. The doctrine which exempts coast fishermen, with their vessels and cargoes, from capture as prizes of war, has been familiar to the United States from the time of the War of Independence, and has been recognized explicitly by the French and British governments. Where there are no treaties and no controlling executive or legislative acts or judicial decisions, as is the case here, resort must be had to the customs and usages of civilized nations, and, as evidence of these, to the works of jurists and commentators, who are well acquainted with the field. Such works are resorted to by judicial tribunals, not for the speculations of their authors concerning what the law ought to be, but for trustworthy evidence of what the law really is. At the present time, by the general consent of the civilized nations of the world, and independently of any express treaty or other public act, it is an established rule of international law that coast fishing vessels, with their implements and supplies, cargoes, and crews, unarmed and honestly pursuing their peaceful calling of catching and bringing in fresh fish, are exempt from capture as prizes of war. Reversed.

ANALYSIS

In a dissenting opinion, which was not included in the casebook excerpt, Chief Justice Fuller argued that the captured vessels were of such a size and range as to not fall within the exemption. The Chief Justice also contended that the exemption in any case had not become a customary rule of international law, but was only an act of grace that had not been authorized by the President.

Quicknotes

CONDEMNATION The taking of private property for public use so long as just compensation is paid therefor.

Filartiga v. Pena-Irala

Father of decedent (P) v. Inspector general (D)

630 F.2d 876 (2d Cir. 1980).

NATURE OF CASE: Appeal of dismissal of wrongful death action.

FACT SUMMARY: Filartiga (P) filed an action against Pena-Irala (D), contending he had tortured to death Filartiga's (P) decedent.

RULE OF LAW

Torture may be considered to violate the law of nations for purposes of the Alien Tort Statute.

FACTS: Seventeen-year-old Joelito Filartiga was kidnapped and tortured to death by Pena-Irala (D), who was then Inspector General of Police in Asuncion, Paraguay. Filartiga (P) claimed that Joelito was tortured and killed in retaliation for his father's political activities and beliefs, which were against the Paraguayan government. Filartiga (P) brought suit in Paraguay against Pena (D) and the police for the murder of his son, but his attorney was arrested and tortured, and later disbarred without cause. During this proceeding, another man, Hugo Duarte, confessed to the murder. He was never convicted or sentenced. Filartiga (P) believed the evidence showed that his son was professionally tortured, and that Duarte had nothing to do with the murder. Pena-Irala (D) came to the United States in July 1978 and stayed beyond his visa. Dolly Filartiga, Joelito's brother, who had been living in Washington, D.C., found out about his presence and informed Immigration and Naturalization Service (INS) of their illegal presence. They were slated for deportation when Filartiga (P) brought an action against Pena-Irala (D), claiming that he had tortured to death Filartiga's (P) decedent while Pena-Irala (D) was police Inspector-General. All parties were Paraguayan citizens. Jurisdiction was based on the Alien Tort Statute, 28 U.S.C. § 1350, which provided jurisdiction for torts committed in violation of "the law of nations." The district court dismissed for lack of jurisdiction. Filartiga (P) appealed.

ISSUE: May torture be considered to violate the law of nations for purposes of the Alien Tort Statute?

HOLDING AND DECISION: (Kaufman, J.) Yes. Torture may be considered to violate the law of nations for purposes of the Alien Tort Statute. The prohibition against torture has become part of customary international law. This is particularly evidenced by various United Nations declarations, such as the Universal Declaration of Human Rights and the 1975 Declaration on the Protection of all Persons from Torture. A declaration from the United Nations is a formal and solemn instrument, and can be considered an authoritative statement from the international community. Beyond that, torture has been officially renounced in the vast majority of nations. For these reasons, this court concludes that torture violates the law of nations. Reversed.

ANALYSIS

It is no great secret that what many members of the United Nations say in their pronouncements and what they do in practice aren't quite the same things. Torture is still widely practiced if not in a majority of countries then in a significant number. Commentators have argued that actual practice, not U.N. declarations, constitute customary international law.

Quicknotes

WRONGFUL DEATH An action brought by the beneficiaries of a deceased person, claiming that the deceased's death was the result of wrongful conduct by the defendant.

Sosa v. Alvarez-Machain

[Parties not identified.]

542 U.S. 692 (2004).

NATURE OF CASE: Appeal of judgment awarding damages to foreign national.

FACT SUMMARY: A Mexican torturer brought suit for damages against the United States and the individual who abducted him and brought him to the United States for trial.

RULE OF LAW

(1) The Alien Tort Statute (ATS) does not create a cause of action for individuals who are victims of violation of international law.

(2) Abduction of a foreign national from his country for criminal trial in the United States does not support a claim against the U.S. government under the Federal Tort Claims Act.

FACTS: Enrique Camarena-Salazar was an agent of the Drug Enforcement Administration (DEA), and was captured while on assignment in Mexico. He was tortured over two days, and then murdered. Humberto Alvarez-Machain (P), a Mexican physician, acted to prolong Camarena-Salazar's life in order to extend the interrogation and torture. A U.S. federal grand jury indicted Alvarez (P) for the torture and murder, and a federal district court issued a warrant for his arrest. The Mexican government would not help get Alvarez (P) to the United States, so the DEA hired Jose Francisco Sosa (D) to abduct him. Once in American custody, Alvarez (P) moved to dismiss the indictment on grounds that his seizure violated the extradition treaty between the United States and Mexico. The district court agreed and the Ninth Circuit Court of Appeals affirmed. The United States Supreme Court reversed, holding that Alvarez's (P) forcible seizure did not affect the jurisdiction of the federal court. The case was tried, and at its end the district court granted Alvarez's (P) motion for acquittal. Alvarez (P) went back to Mexico and filed a claim seeking damages from the United States under the Federal Torts Claim Act (FTCA), alleging false arrest, and from Sosa (D) under the Alien Tort Statute (ATS), for violation of the law of nations. The district court dismissed the claim against the United States, but awarded summary judgment and $25,000 in damages to Alvarez on the ATS claim against Sosa (D). The Ninth Circuit affirmed the ATS judgment, but reversed the dismissal of the FTCA claim, on grounds that the DEA had no authority to abduct Alvarez.

ISSUE:

(1) Does the Alien Tort Statute create a cause of action for individuals who are victims of violation of international law?

(2) Does abduction of a foreign national from his country for criminal trial in the United States support a claim against the U.S. government under the Federal Tort Claims Act?

HOLDING AND DECISION: (Souter, J.)

(1) No. The Alien Tort Statute does not create a cause of action for individuals who are victims of violation of international law. The statute was intended to be exclusively concerned with jurisdiction, in the sense of addressing the power of courts to entertain cases concerned with a certain subject. The common law indicates that the ATS conferred jurisdiction for a relatively modest set of cases, alleging violations of the traditional law of nations, including only offenses against ambassadors, violations of safe conduct, and individual actions arising out of prize captures and piracy. There is no record of congressional discussion about private actions that might be subject to ATS's jurisdictional provision, or about any need for further legislation to create private remedies. While no legal development has categorically precluded federal courts from recognizing a claim under international law as an element of common law, the discretion accorded federal courts in fashioning such claims should be restrained. Therefore, courts should require any claim based on present day international law to rest on a norm of international character accepted by the civilized world and defined with specificity.

(2) No. Abduction of a foreign national from his country for criminal trial in the United States does not support a claim against the U.S. government under the Federal Tort Claims Act. [Discussion of the FTCA claims was omitted from the casebook excerpt.] Reversed.

CONCURRENCE: (Scalia, J.) While the holding that the ATS is a jurisdictional statute creating no new causes of action is correct, federal courts do not enjoy any level of discretion in considering new causes of action. While it is true that no development between the enactment of the ATS in 1789 and the birth of modern international human rights litigation under that statute in 1980 has precluded federal courts from recognizing a claim under international law, the proper question is not whether any case or congressional action prevents federal courts from applying the law of nations as part of the general common law, but what authorizes that exception from fundamental precedent holding that a general common law does not exist.

Continued on next page.

CONCURRENCE: (Breyer, J.) The enforcement of an international norm by one nation's courts implies that other nations' courts may do the same. Therefore, exercise of jurisdiction under the ATS would have to be consistent with notions of comity that lead each nation to respect the sovereignty of other nations by limiting the reach of its laws and their enforcement.

ANALYSIS

The events giving rise to this case are twenty years old. This was the first and last time the Supreme Court addressed the scope of the ATS. According to this decision, then, federal courts might still recognize an individual cause of action under the ATS.

Quicknotes

FEDERAL TORT CLAIMS ACT (FTCA) Legislation that provides a limited waiver of the federal government's sovereign immunity when its employees are negligent within the scope of their employment.

Crosby v. National Foreign Trade Council

State (D) v. Trade association (P)

530 U.S. 363 (2000).

NATURE OF CASE: Appeal from decision that a state law that bars state entities from buying goods or services from companies doing business with a certain nation violates the Supremacy Clause where Congress has passed a statute that imposes mandatory and conditional sanctions on that nation.

FACT SUMMARY: Massachusetts passed a law barring state entities from buying goods or services from companies doing business with Burma. Subsequently, Congress imposed mandatory and conditional sanctions on Burma. An action was brought claiming the state statute was invalid under the Supremacy Clause of the Constitution owing to its threat of frustrating federal statutory objectives.

RULE OF LAW

A state law that bars state entities from buying goods or services from companies doing business with a certain nation violates the Supremacy Clause where Congress has passed a statute that imposes mandatory and conditional sanctions on that nation.

FACTS: In 1996, Massachusetts (D) passed a law, "An Act Regulating State Contracts with Companies Doing Business with or in Burma (Myanmar)," barring state entities from buying goods or services from companies doing business with Burma (Myanmar). Three months later, Congress passed a statute imposing mandatory and conditional sanctions on Burma. The statute, among other things, authorized the President to impose sanctions in addition to those specified in the statute upon findings of human rights violations and other conditions, and directed the President to work to develop a strategy for bringing democracy to, and improving human rights practices in, Burma. Congress also called for Presidential cooperation with members of the Association of Southeast Asian Nations (ASEAN) and other countries in developing such a strategy, directed the President to encourage a dialogue between the government of Burma and the democratic opposition, and required him to report to the Congress on the progress of these diplomatic efforts. The statute authorized the President to waive any sanctions under the act if he determined and certified to Congress that the application of such sanction would be contrary to the national security interests of the United States. In May 1997, the President certified that the Burmese government had committed large-scale repression of the democratic opposition in Burma, and found that this constituted an extraordinary threat to the national security of the United States, tantamount to a national emergency. The President then prohibited new investment in Burma by United States persons. The Massachusetts statute was challenged as violating the Supremacy Clause owing to its threat of frustrating federal statutory objectives.

ISSUE: Does a state law that bars state entities from buying goods or services from companies doing business with a certain nation violate the Supremacy Clause where Congress has passed a statute that imposes mandatory and conditional sanctions on that nation?

HOLDING AND DECISION: (Souter, J.) Yes. A state law that bars state entities from buying goods or services from companies doing business with a certain nation violates the Supremacy Clause where Congress has passed a statute that imposes mandatory and conditional sanctions on that nation. Even without an express preemption provision, state law must yield to a congressional Act if Congress intends to occupy the field, or to the extent of any conflict with a federal statute. The Court will find preemption where it is impossible for a private party to comply with both state and federal law, and where the state law is an obstacle to the accomplishment and execution of Congress's full purposes and objectives. What is a sufficient obstacle is determined by examining the federal statute and identifying its purpose and intended effects. First, the state Act is an obstacle to the federal Act's delegation of discretion to the President to control economic sanctions against Burma. Although Congress put initial sanctions in place, it authorized the President to terminate the measures upon certifying that Burma has made progress in human rights and democracy, to impose new sanctions upon findings of repression, and, most importantly, to suspend sanctions in the interest of national security. The breadth of executive branch authority controls the preemption issue here. The President has the authority not merely to make a political statement but to achieve a political result, and the fullness of his authority shows the importance in the congressional mind of reaching that result. Yet the state Act's sanctions are immediate and perpetual, and therefore undermine the President's authority by leaving him with less economic and diplomatic leverage than the federal Act permits; the state Act stands as an obstacle to the accomplishment and execution of the full purposes and objectives of Congress. Second, the state Act interferes with Congress's intention to limit economic pressure against the Burmese Government to a specific range. It prohibits some contracts permitted by the federal Act, affects more investment than the federal Act, and reaches foreign and domestic companies, whereas

Continued on next page.

the federal Act confines its reach to United States persons. It thus conflicts with the federal law by penalizing individuals and conduct that Congress has explicitly exempted or excluded from sanctions. Finally, the state Act is at odds with the President's authority to speak for the United States among the world's nations to develop a comprehensive, multilateral Burma strategy. Congress called for Presidential cooperation with other countries in developing such a strategy, directed the President to encourage a dialogue between the Burmese Government and the democratic opposition, and required him to report to Congress on these efforts. This delegation of power, like that over economic sanctions, invested the President with the maximum authority of the National Government. The state Act undermines the President's capacity for effective diplomacy. In response to its passage, foreign governments have filed formal protests with the National Government and lodged formal complaints against the United States in the World Trade Organization (WTO). The State's remaining argument—that Congress's failure to preempt state and local sanctions demonstrates implicit permission—is unavailing. The existence of a conflict cognizable under the Supremacy Clause does not depend on express congressional recognition that federal and state law may conflict, and a failure to provide for preemption expressly may reflect nothing more than the settled character of implied preemption that courts will dependably apply. Affirmed.

ANALYSIS

Although the Court found dormant foreign affairs preemption here, it did so because it found that the state law was an obstacle to the accomplishment of the intended purpose and natural effect of the federal law in several significant ways. However, such "obstacle" conflict preemption will not be found because state law is simply in general tension with broad or abstract goals that may be attributed to various federal laws or programs.

Quicknotes

PREEMPTION Doctrine holding that matters of national interest take precedence over matters of local interest; the federal law takes precedence over state law.

SUPREMACY CLAUSE Article VI of the U.S. Constitution, which provides that federal action must prevail over inconsistent state action.

American Insurance Association v. Garamendi

Insurance association v. State of California

539 U.S. 396 (2003).

NATURE OF CASE: Appeal to United States Supreme Court by insurance association and United States as amicus curiae of ruling in favor of the state of California.

FACT SUMMARY: A California law required insurance companies (P) doing business in the state (D) to disclose prior issuance of Holocaust-era insurance policies in Europe.

RULE OF LAW

The likelihood that state legislation will produce something more than incidental effect on foreign affairs requires preemption of the state law by national policy, even when there is no affirmative federal activity in the subject area of the state law, and therefore no showing of conflict.

FACTS: A California law required insurance companies (P) doing business in the state (D) to disclose prior issuance of Holocaust-era insurance policies in Europe.

ISSUE: Does the likelihood that state legislation will produce something more than incidental effect on foreign affairs require preemption of the state law by national policy, even when there is no affirmative federal activity in the subject area of the state law, and therefore no showing of conflict?

HOLDING AND DECISION: (Souter, J.) Yes. The likelihood that state legislation will produce something more than incidental effect on foreign affairs requires preemption of the state law by national policy, even when there is no affirmative federal activity in the subject area of the state law, and therefore no showing of conflict. California's provision of regulatory sanctions to compel disclosure of certain information by insurance companies contravenes national foreign policy encouraging European governments and companies to volunteer disclosure. And even if there were no conflict here, California's interest in vindicating the claims of Holocaust survivors living in the state is weak compared with the national interest in vindicating the claims of Holocaust survivors throughout the country. California seeks to use "an iron fist" where the President has consistently chosen "kid gloves." Reversed.

DISSENT: (Ginsburg, J.) Because no executive agreement or other formal expression of foreign policy disapproves state disclosure laws like the one at issue here, California's law should be left intact. The notion of "dormant foreign affairs preemption" should be limited to situations in which the state law criticizes foreign governments. The state law at issue here takes no position on any foreign government. In addition, declining to invalidate the California state law in this case would reserve foreign affairs preemption for circumstances where the President, acting under statutory or constitutional authority, has spoken clearly on the issue.

ANALYSIS

This case essentially preempts any state law that deals in any way with international relations. The majority's broad strokes prevent the formulation of a rule that outlines what a state may and may not do in a state law that has any possible bearing on international relations.

Quicknotes

AMICUS CURIAE A third party, not implicated in the suit, which seeks to file a brief containing information for the court's consideration in conformity with its position.

PREEMPTION Doctrine holding that matters of national interest take precedence over matters of local interest; the federal law takes precedence over state law.

CHAPTER 4

International Dispute Resolution

Quick Reference Rules of Law

PAGE

1. **Jurisdiction Under a Dispute Settlement Clause in a Treaty.** The International Court of Justice (ICJ) has jurisdiction to hear disputes about the interpretation or application of a treaty, if that treaty contains an ICJ dispute resolution clause. (Oil Platforms (Islamic Republic of Iran v. United States of America)) *30*

2. **Jurisdiction Under the Optional Clause.** The jurisdiction of the International Court of Justice (ICJ) over a dispute between two nations is limited by the extent to which their declarations accepting compulsory jurisdiction of the ICJ overlap in conferring it. (Certain Norwegian Loans (France v. Norway)) *31*

3. **Jurisdiction Under the Optional Clause.** (1) If notification of a modification to a declaration accepting compulsory jurisdiction of the International Court of Justice (ICJ) does not follow the declaration's guidelines for such modification, the notification does not operate to remove the ICJ's jurisdiction. (2) The U.S. declaration effectively provides the necessary consent of the United States to the jurisdiction of the ICJ in the case against Nicaragua even if the declaration provides that ICJ's jurisdiction shall not extend to disputes arising under a multilateral treaty. (Military and Paramilitary Activities In and Against Nicaragua (Nicaragua v. United States of America)) *32*

4. **Procedure in the International Court of Justice—Admissibility.** The application of Nicaragua is not inadmissible because it deals with the politically sensitive use of force issues that are not judicial in nature. (Military and Paramilitary Activities In and Against Nicaragua (Nicaragua v. United States of America)) *34*

5. **The Relationship of European Union Law to National Law.** The European Economic Community Treaty, which came into force in 1958, created individual rights in the nationals of member states which may be asserted in the domestic courts of those states. (Van Gend en Loos v. Nederlandse Administratie der Belastingen) *35*

6. **The Supremacy of Union Law and the Restriction of National Powers.** When national law conflicts with Community law, national courts must give full and immediate effect to Community law. (Administrazione delle Finanze dello Stato v. Simmenthal S.p.A.) *36*

7. **Judicial Attitudes Toward International Arbitration.** An arbitration clause in an international trade agreement is enforceable in an antitrust context. (Mitsubishi Motors Corp. v. Soler Chrysler-Plymouth) *37*

8. **Enforcement of Arbitral Awards—Under the New York Convention.** A foreign arbitral award may be confirmed by a U.S. court. (Parsons & Whittemore Overseas Co. v. Société Générale de l'Industrie du Papier (RAKTA)) *38*

Oil Platforms (Islamic Republic of Iran v. United States of America)

Treaty partner (P) v. Treaty partner (D)

Int'l. Ct. of Justice, 1996 I.C.J. 803 (December 12, 1996).

NATURE OF CASE: Dispute over jurisdiction of the International Court of Justice.

FACT SUMMARY: The United States (D) destroyed several Iranian oil production platforms in the Persian Gulf. Iran challenged U.S. actions, arguing that the International Court of Justice (ICJ) had jurisdiction through the dispute resolution clause in Article XXI of the 1955 U.S.-Iran Treaty of Amity. The United States (D) argued that the ICJ did not have jurisdiction, and that the law regulating the use of force and self-defense governed the dispute.

RULE OF LAW

The International Court of Justice (ICJ) has jurisdiction to hear disputes about the interpretation or application of a treaty, if that treaty contains an ICJ dispute resolution clause.

FACTS: The United States (D) destroyed several Iranian oil production platforms in the Persian Gulf during the Iran-Iraq war in 1988. Iran (P) had been attacking ships engaged in commercial trade with Arab Persian Gulf countries, which, though they formally retained neutral status, Iran viewed as supporting Iraq. The United States (D) concluded that Iran (P) was using the oil platforms as command centers for Iranian attacks against the neutral commercial vessels, and destroyed the platforms to ensure that commercial shipping in the Gulf was not interrupted. Iran (P) challenged U.S. actions, arguing that they violated the 1955 U.S.-Iran Treaty of Amity, and that the International Court of Justice (ICJ) had jurisdiction through the dispute resolution clause in Article XXI of the Treaty. Iran (P) argued that the United States (D) violated three articles of the Treaty: Article I, which provided that there "shall be firm and enduring peace and sincere friendship between the United States of America and Iran" ; Article IV(1), which provided that the parties "shall at all times accord fair and equitable treatment to nationals and companies of the other High Contracting Party, and to their property and enterprises;" and Article X(1), which provided that there "shall be freedom of commerce and navigation" between the territories of the two parties. The United States (D) argued that the attacks on the platforms did not fall within the scope of the Treaty in general, and specifically Article X, because the term "commerce" (1) was confined to maritime commerce, (2) was limited to commerce between the United States and Iran, and (3) referred solely to the actual sale or exchange of goods. The United States (D) argued that the ICJ therefore did not have jurisdiction, and that the law regulating the use of force and self-defense governed the dispute.

ISSUE: Does the ICJ have jurisdiction to hear disputes about the interpretation or application of a treaty, if that treaty contains an ICJ dispute resolution clause?

HOLDING AND DECISION: [Judge not stated in casebook excerpt.] Yes. The ICJ has jurisdiction to hear disputes about the interpretation or application of a treaty, if that treaty contains an ICJ dispute resolution clause. The U.S.-Iran Treaty of Amity provides that the ICJ has jurisdiction over the interpretation or applicability of the Treaty. In order to answer a question about the interpretation or application of the Treaty, however, the ICJ first had to determine whether the Treaty covered the destruction of the platforms and whether, as a result, the dispute was one the ICJ had jurisdiction to resolve under Article XII. Article I states only an objective of the Treaty, and as such does not cover the actions carried out by the United States (D) against Iran (P). Similarly, Article IV, paragraph 1, concerns the treatment by each party of the nationals and companies of the other party, as well as their property and enterprises, and as such does not cover the actions carried out by the United States (D) against Iran (P). Article X, paragraph 1, however, covers actions that might affect "commerce" between the parties, and as such covers the actions taken by the United States (D) against Iran (P). Contrary to U.S. arguments, "commerce" taken in its ordinary sense or in its legal meaning, and at a domestic or international level, has broader meaning than the mere reference to purchase and sale. Rather, "commerce" includes commercial activities in general and the ancillary activities related to commerce. Thus, the destruction of the platforms was capable of having an adverse effect upon the freedom of commerce as guaranteed by Article X, paragraph 1, of the Treaty, and the ICJ has jurisdiction to evaluate its lawfulness in the context of that paragraph.

ANALYSIS

The ICJ determined that the United States' actions violated the Treaty before determining whether it had jurisdiction to make that determination. In a sense, before it even ruled that it had jurisdiction, it reached the merits and decided in Iran's favor, even though not formally. The ICJ would reach the merits judgment in the case seven years later, and found in favor of the United States.

Quicknotes

JURISDICTION The authority of a court to hear and declare judgment in respect to a particular matter.

Certain Norwegian Loans (France v. Norway)

French government (P) v. Norwegian government (D)

Int'l. Ct. of Justice, 1957 I.C.J. 9 (July 6, 1957).

NATURE OF CASE: Action to secure payment on Norwegian bonds.

FACT SUMMARY: France (P) believed that Norwegian bonds held by French nationals should have been redeemed in gold. Norway (D) disagreed. France (P) accepted compulsory jurisdiction of the International Court of Justice to resolve the dispute, but limited its acceptance to matters that did not fall within national jurisdiction, which France (P) alone would identify. Norway's (D) acceptance was unconditional.

RULE OF LAW

The jurisdiction of the International Court of Justice (ICJ) over a dispute between two nations is limited by the extent to which their declarations accepting compulsory jurisdiction of the ICJ overlap in conferring it.

FACTS: Norway (D) issued bonds before World War I that certain French nationals purchased, which France (P) claimed guaranteed payment in gold. Norway (D) later passed legislation allowing payment of the bonds with bank notes, which were not convertible to gold. The French government (P) attempted to bring the claim of its nationals into international dispute resolution, but the Norwegian government (D) claimed that the matter was within Norway's jurisdiction. The French government (P) brought the case to the International Court of Justice (ICJ), and both parties declared their acceptance of the compulsory jurisdiction of the ICJ under Article 36(2). The French declaration was conditional, in that it did not apply to differences related to matters that are within France's national jurisdiction as understood by the French government (P). Norway's (D) declaration was unconditional, but Norway (D) argued that France's (P) rights to retain jurisdiction should not be greater than Norway's (D).

ISSUE: Is jurisdiction of the ICJ over a dispute between two nations limited by the extent to which their declarations accepting compulsory jurisdiction of the ICJ overlap in conferring it?

HOLDING AND DECISION: [Judges not stated in casebook excerpt.] Yes. The jurisdiction of the ICJ over a dispute between two nations is limited by the extent to which their declarations accepting compulsory jurisdiction of the ICJ overlap in conferring it. France (P) limited acceptance of the compulsory jurisdiction of the ICJ by excluding disputes "relating to matters which are essentially within the national jurisdiction as understood by the Government of the French Republic." Norway (D) is equally entitled to accept from the compulsory jurisdiction of the ICJ disputes understood by Norway (D) to be essentially within its national jurisdiction, even though it did not limit its declaration accepting compulsory jurisdiction as France (P) did. The French declaration accepts the ICJ's jurisdiction within narrower limits than the Norwegian declaration, and the common will of the parties, on which the ICJ's jurisdiction rests, exists within the narrower limits set by France. Because Norway (D) claimed the matter falls within Norway's jurisdiction, the ICJ lacked jurisdiction to hear the matter.

ANALYSIS

Note that the condition of reciprocity requires that a reservation in a declaration accepting compulsory jurisdiction of the ICJ by one nation operates to grant the opposing nation the same reservation. The condition of reciprocity applies not only to reservations, but to expiration dates on declarations, unilateral amendments of declarations, and virtually any other unilateral action by a state to limit the ICJ's jurisdiction.

Quicknotes

JURISDICTION The authority of a court to hear and declare judgment in respect to a particular matter.

Military and Paramilitary Activities In and Against Nicaragua (Nicaragua v. United States of America)

Complaining nation (P) v. Alleged wrongdoer (D)

Int'l. Ct. of Justice, 1984 I.C.J. 392 (Preliminary Objections Judgment of Nov. 26, 1984).

NATURE OF CASE: Dispute over jurisdiction of the International Court of Justice.

FACT SUMMARY: The United States (D) had accepted the International Court of Justice's (ICJ's) jurisdiction through a declaration, reserving the right to modify its declaration, with the stipulation that the modification would take place six months after it was made. Just as Nicaragua (P) was filing charges against the United States (D) in the ICJ, the United States (D) notified the UN that it exempted from ICJ jurisdiction actions by Central American states, effective immediately.

RULE OF LAW

(1) If notification of a modification to a declaration accepting compulsory jurisdiction of the International Court of Justice (ICJ) does not follow the declaration's guidelines for such modification, the notification does not operate to remove the ICJ's jurisdiction.

(2) The U.S. declaration effectively provides the necessary consent of the United States to the jurisdiction of the ICJ in the case against Nicaragua, even if the declaration provides that ICJ's jurisdiction shall not extend to disputes arising under a multilateral treaty.

FACTS: Nicaragua (P) and the United States (D) accepted compulsory jurisdiction of the International Court of Justice (ICJ). A 1946 declaration by the United States (D) accepted compulsory jurisdiction of the ICJ with the reservation that the United States (D) could modify or terminate it upon six months notice. Nicaragua's (P) declaration, dated 1929, originally applied to the Permanent Court of International Justice, and was unconditional. Nicaragua (P) ratified it in 1939, but it did not acquire binding force immediately because the document never reached the League of Nations, possibly because it had been lost at sea during World War II. In any event, Nicaragua (P) became a party to the statute of the new ICJ and expressly refrained from limiting the declaration, and it was considered by the ICJ to be valid. On April 6, 1984, the United States (D) notified the UN that disputes with Central American states were excluded from the coverage of the 1946 declaration, effective immediately, therefore not providing the six-month notice the declaration promised. On April 9, 1984, Nicaragua (P) filed a claim against the United States (D) for conducting military and paramilitary activities in and against Nicaragua.

ISSUE:

(1) If notification of a modification to a declaration accepting compulsory jurisdiction of the ICJ does not follow the declaration's guidelines for such modification, does the notification operate to remove the ICJ's jurisdiction?

(2) Does the U.S. declaration effectively provide the necessary consent of the United States to the jurisdiction of the ICJ in the case against Nicaragua, if the declaration provides that ICJ's jurisdiction shall not extend to disputes arising under a multilateral treaty?

HOLDING AND DECISION: [Judge not stated in casebook excerpt.]

(1) No. If notification of a modification to a declaration accepting compulsory jurisdiction of the ICJ does not follow the declaration's guidelines for such modification, the notification does not operate to remove the ICJ's jurisdiction. The U.S. notice of termination does not nullify the U.S. declaration accepting compulsory jurisdiction of the IJC with respect to Central American states, because the United States (D) failed to provide six months notice of the modification, a formality it agreed to in the declaration. The unilateral nature of declaration does not mean that the state making the declaration is free to amend the scope and contents of its commitments to other states accepting the jurisdiction of the ICJ as it pleases. The principle of reciprocity cannot be invoked to excuse departure from the U.S.'s own declaration, because reciprocity is concerned with the scope and substance of the commitments entered into, and does not relate to the formal conditions of their creation, duration, or extinction. Further, the United States (D) acted only three days before Nicaragua's (P) application, which is not a reasonable period of notice of termination. The six months' notice clause forms an important part of the United States declaration and it is a condition that must be complied with in case of either termination or modification, and it therefore cannot override the obligation of the United States to submit to the jurisdiction of the Court with Nicaragua (P).

(2) Yes. The U.S. declaration effectively provides the necessary consent of the United States to the jurisdiction of the ICJ in the case against Nicaragua, even if the declaration provides that ICJ's jurisdiction shall not extend to disputes arising under a multilateral treaty. The

Continued on next page.

multilateral treaty reservation could not bar adjudication by the ICJ of all of Nicaragua's (P) claims because Nicaragua (P) does not confine those claims only to violations of four multilateral conventions. Nicaragua (P) claims in its application multiple violations by the United States (D) of general and customary international law. The ICJ would not dismiss Nicaragua's claims simply because they are part of the treaties. The ICJ therefore has jurisdiction to hear the claim filed by Nicaragua as it concerns the interpretation or application of the Treaty of Friendship, Commerce and Navigation between the United States (D) and Nicaragua (P).

ANALYSIS

Less than two months after the ICJ decided that it had jurisdiction in this case, the United States announced that it had decided not to participate in further proceedings in the case. Despite the withdrawal of the United States, the ICJ continued the proceedings, and less than a year later, the United States gave notice that it was terminating its 1946 declaration of acceptance of the ICJ's compulsory jurisdiction.

Quicknotes

JURISDICTION The authority of a court to hear and declare judgment in respect to a particular matter.

Military and Paramilitary Activities In and Against Nicaragua (Nicaragua v. United States of America)

Complaining nation (P) v. Alleged wrongdoer (D)

Int'l. Ct. of Justice, 1984 I.C.J. 392 (Preliminary Objections Judgment of May 10, 1984).

NATURE OF CASE: Dispute over jurisdiction of the International Court of Justice.

FACT SUMMARY: [The United States (D) had accepted the International Court of Justice's (ICJ's) jurisdiction through a declaration, reserving the right to modify its declaration, with the stipulation that the modification would take place six months after it was made. Just as Nicaragua (P) was filing charges against the United States (D) in the ICJ, the United States (D) notified the UN that it exempted from ICJ jurisdiction actions by Central American states, effective immediately.]

RULE OF LAW

The application of Nicaragua is not inadmissible because it deals with the politically sensitive use of force issues that are not judicial in nature.

FACTS: [Nicaragua (P) and the United States (D) accepted compulsory jurisdiction of the International Court of Justice (ICJ). A 1946 declaration by the United States (D) accepted compulsory jurisdiction of the ICJ with the reservation that the United States (D) could modify or terminate it upon six months notice. Nicaragua's (P) declaration, dated 1929, originally applied to the Permanent Court of International Justice, and was unconditional. Nicaragua (P) ratified it in 1939, but it did not acquire binding force immediately because the document never reached the League of Nations, possibly because it had been lost at sea during World War II. In any event, Nicaragua (P) became a party to the statute of the new ICJ and expressly refrained from limiting the declaration, and it was considered by the ICJ to be valid. On April 6, 1984, the United States (D) notified the UN that disputes with Central American states were excluded from the coverage of the 1946 declaration, effective immediately, therefore not providing the six-month notice the declaration promised. On April 9, 1984, Nicaragua (P) filed a claim against the United States (D) for conducting military and paramilitary activities in and against Nicaragua.]

ISSUE: Is the application of Nicaragua inadmissible because it deals with politically sensitive use of force issues that are not judicial in nature?

HOLDING AND DECISION: [Judge not stated in casebook excerpt.] No. The application of Nicaragua is not inadmissible because it deals with politically sensitive use of force issues that are not judicial in nature. The fact that the case might also be under review by the UN Security Council does not mean it cannot also be under review in the ICJ. The Charter of the United Nations does not confer exclusive responsibility on the Security Council for purposes such as Nicaragua's. Moreover, the ICJ will not shy away from a case merely because it has political implications or because it involves the use of force.

ANALYSIS

In 1986, the ICJ ruled against the United States on the merits, deciding that it had violated customary international law and its Treaty of Friendship, Commerce and Navigation with Nicaragua. The United States continued to decline to participate in the proceedings. In 1990, after a new Nicaraguan regime came to power, the United States pressured Nicaragua to renounce all rights of actions based on the case.

Quicknotes

JURISDICTION The authority of a court to hear and declare judgment in respect to a particular matter.

Van Gend en Loos v. Nederlandse Administratie der Belastingen

Importer (P) v. Dutch customs collector (D)

European Ct. of Justice, Case 26/62, [1963] ECR 1.

NATURE OF CASE: Request for ruling on standing of nationals to assert European Economic Community created claims.

FACT SUMMARY: Van Gend en Loos (P) imported urea formaldehyde into Holland from Germany, but the product was subjected to an eight percent duty despite a limitation on import duties in the European Economic Community Treaty to three percent.

RULE OF LAW

The European Economic Community Treaty, which came into force in 1958, created individual rights in the nationals of member states which may be asserted in the domestic courts of those states.

FACTS: Van Gend en Loos (P) imported urea formaldehyde into Holland from Germany in 1960. In 1958, the European Economic Community (EEC) Treaty came into force; its Article 12 prohibited member states from introducing new duties on imports and from increasing existing duties. Nevertheless, in 1958 a protocol between Holland, Luxembourg, and Belgium subjected all imports to an eight percent duty. Van Gend en Loos (P) contended that the preexisting duty limited by the EEC Treaty was three percent, although a question of fact remained whether the preexisting duty was in fact ten percent (and thus the eight percent did not represent a real increase in the tariff). Van Gend en Loos (P) filed a suit challenging the imposition of the eight percent duty by the Nederlandse Administratie Der Belastingen (D), the Dutch customs collectors, in the Tariefcommissie, the Dutch court. The Tariefcommissie in turn certified questions for preliminary rulings by the Court of Justice, including: (1) whether nationals of an EEC member state can assert in domestic courts individual rights created by the EEC treaty; and (2) whether the eight percent duty violated Article 12 of the EEC treaty.

ISSUE: Did the European Economic Community Treaty create individual rights in the nationals of member states which might be asserted in the domestic courts of those states?

HOLDING AND DECISION: [Judge not stated in casebook excerpt.] Yes. The European Economic Community (EEC) Treaty, which entered into force in 1958, created individual rights in the nationals of member states which may be asserted in the domestic courts of those states. The objective of the EEC Treaty implies that it is more than an agreement which merely creates mutual obligations between the contracting states; its preamble instead refers not only to governments but to peoples. The EEC constitutes a new legal order of international law for the benefit of which the states have limited their sovereign rights, and the subjects of which comprise not only member states but also their nationals. Thus, Van de Gend en Loos (D) has standing to challenge the imposition of the percent tariff in the Dutch courts. As to whether the eight percent duty violated Article 12 of the EEC treaty, it is up to the Tariefcommissie to determine whether the import duty charged Van Gend en Loos (P) was higher after 1958 than before.

ANALYSIS

Written EEC law contains no guidelines concerning whether the law of member states prevails over the EEC law in cases of conflict. Interestingly, such conflict might have been avoided had EEC written law contained a "supremacy clause" like that contained in the United States Constitution. Note also that "customary law," which encompasses general principles of international law, is considered a supplementary source of community law.

Quicknotes

SUPREMACY CLAUSE Article VI, Sec. 2, of the Constitution, which provides that federal action must prevail over inconsistent state action.

Amministrazione delle Finanze dello Stato v. Simmenthal S.p.A.

Italian government (D) v. Beef importer (P)

European Ct. of Justice, Case 106/77, [1978] E.C.R. 629.

NATURE OF CASE: Appeal from order of import fee refund.

FACT SUMMARY: The Italian government (D) appealed an Italian court order refunding the Italian import fee imposed by Italian legislation on inspections of beef imported for human consumption.

RULE OF LAW

When national law conflicts with Community law, national courts must give full and immediate effect to Community law.

FACTS: The Italian government (D) charged Simmenthal (P) a fee for inspections of beef he imported for human consumption. Simmenthal (P) sued in Italian court, claiming the fees were contrary to Community law. The Italian court referred the question to the European Court of Justice (ECJ), which ruled that the fees were invalid under Community law. When the Italian court ordered a refund, the Italian government (D) appealed, claiming the Italian court was bound by Italian law absent parliamentary or constitutional legislation. The Italian court referred the issue again to the ECJ.

ISSUE: When national law conflicts with Community law, must national courts give full and immediate effect to Community law?

HOLDING AND DECISION: [Judge not stated in casebook excerpt.] Yes. To give effect to the obligations and rights agreed upon by signatories to the European Economic Treaty, the provisions of the treaty must automatically render inapplicable any conflicting national law of member states. The adoption of any new national measures is also precluded to the extent that they would be incompatible with Community law provisions. A national court must therefore refuse on its own motion to apply any provision of national legislation that conflicts with Community law and need not wait for legislative or other constitutional repeal of offending legislation. Accordingly, the Italian court was correct, and the Italian government's (D) appeal must be rejected.

ANALYSIS

Unlike traditional international treaties, the EEC Treaty creates an independent legal system binding on members. Within certain fields, signatory nations agree to limit their national legal systems. Article 219 of the EEC Treaty limits the methods of resolving disputes among member states to procedures enumerated in the treaty.

Mitsubishi Motors Corp. v. Soler Chrysler-Plymouth

Manufacturer (P) v. Dealer (D)

473 U.S. 614 (1985).

NATURE OF CASE: Review of order invalidating arbitration clause in antitrust dispute arising in an international transaction.

FACT SUMMARY: Soler Chrysler-Plymouth (D) contended that an arbitration clause in an international trade agreement was unenforceable in an antitrust context.

RULE OF LAW

An arbitration clause in an international trade agreement is enforceable in an antitrust context.

FACTS: Soler Chrysler-Plymouth, Inc. (D) signed a dealership agreement with Mitsubishi Motors Corp. (P), a Japanese corporation, for the former to sell autos, manufactured by Mitsubishi (P), in the Puerto Rico market. Relations between Soler (D) and Mitsubishi (P) degenerated over time, and Mitsubishi (P) eventually filed a breach of contract action in U.S. district court. Soler (D) counterclaimed, raising, among other claims, certain antitrust claims. Mitsubishi (P) filed a motion to enforce an arbitration clause in the distribution agreement. The district court entered an order mandating arbitration. The court of appeals reversed, holding such clauses unenforceable in an antitrust setting. The United States Supreme Court granted review.

ISSUE: Is an arbitration clause in an international trade agreement enforceable in an antitrust context?

HOLDING AND DECISION: (Blackmun, J.) Yes. An arbitration clause in an international trade agreement is enforceable in an antitrust context. As an initial matter, no distinction is to be made regarding the enforceability of arbitration agreements in statutory actions as opposed to those of a non-statutory nature. A party submitting to arbitration does not waive any statutory rights, but merely agrees to an alternate forum. Consequently, absent a statutory prohibition on arbitration agreements, no distinction shall be made between statutory and non-statutory actions. As to the enforceability of an arbitration clause in an international trade contract in the context of antitrust, concerns of international comity, respect for the capacities of foreign and transnational tribunals, and sensitivities to the need of the international commercial system for predictability militate strongly in favor of enforcing such agreements even when they might not be enforced in the domestic context. Further, the Federal Arbitration Act establishes a strong presumption in favor of enforcing arbitration agreements. The concerns raised respecting arbitration of antitrust disputes are (1) the pivotal role private litigants play in enforcing antitrust laws; (2) the danger that such agreements are part of adhesion contracts; (3) the complexity of antitrust issues; and (4) a fear that delegating authority in this area to arbitrators, who are likely to be businesspeople, will be inconsistent with promoting our laws and values. On examination, these concerns are unfounded. As to the first concern, arbitration does not diminish the role of the private litigant, but merely gives him a different forum. As to the second concern, it should not be presumed that such clauses are of an adhesion type; this should be decided in each case individually. Potential complexity should not invalidate arbitration, as the vertical sort of antitrust usually involved in private claims is not as complex as claims of horizontal antitrust. Finally, it is presumptuous to assume that a non-American judicial tribunal is incapable of rendering a just decision. In sum, the concerns against arbitration in an antitrust context do not outweigh the strong presumption in favor thereof. Reversed.

DISSENT: (Stevens, J.) An arbitration clause should not normally be construed to cover a statutory remedy that it does not expressly identify, and Congress did not intend the Federal Arbitration Act to apply to antitrust claims.

ANALYSIS

At common law, there was a strong judicial presumption against arbitration. Numerous reasons for this were given, but the main motivating factor was most likely protection by the courts of what they saw as their "turf." Largely due to court congestion, arbitration is favored today. The existence of the Federal Arbitration Act is an example of this change of attitude.

Quicknotes

ADHESION CONTRACT A contract that is not negotiated by the parties and is usually prepared by the dominant party on a "take it or leave it" basis.

ANTITRUST Body of federal law prohibiting business conduct that constitutes a restraint on trade.

ARBITRATION An agreement to have a dispute heard and decided by a neutral third party, rather than through legal proceedings.

BREACH OF CONTRACT Unlawful failure by a party to perform its obligations pursuant to contract.

COMITY A rule pursuant to which courts in one state give deference to the statutes and judicial decisions of another.

Parsons & Whittemore Overseas Co. v. Société Générale de l'Industrie du Papier (RAKTA)

American corporation (P) v. Egyptian corporation (D)

508 F.2d 969 (2d Cir. 1974).

NATURE OF CASE: Appeal of summary judgment dismissing action to enjoin enforcement of arbitration agreement.

FACT SUMMARY: Société Générale de l'Industrie du Papier (D) sought to enforce a foreign arbitral award.

RULE OF LAW

A foreign arbitral award may be confirmed by a U.S. court.

FACTS: Parsons & Whittemore Overseas Co. (Parsons) (P) contracted with an Egyptian corporation, Société Générale de l'Industrie du Papier (Société) (D), to perform certain construction work in Alexandria, Egypt. The contract contained a clause submitting disputes to an international arbitration tribunal. The contract also contained a standard force majeure clause. Due to political tensions between Egypt and the United States during and subsequent to the 1967 Arab-Israeli Six Day War, most of Parsons's (P) workforce left Egypt, and it was unable to complete its work. Société (D) contended that the contract had been breached; Parsons (P) contended that its performance had been excused under the force majeure clause. Pursuant to the contract, the matter was submitted to a three-member arbitration tribunal. The tribunal awarded $312,507 to Société (D). Parsons (P) filed an action to enjoin collection; Société counterclaimed to confirm the award. The U.S. district court granted summary judgment confirming the award, and Parsons (P) appealed.

ISSUE: May a foreign arbitral award be confirmed by a U.S. court?

HOLDING AND DECISION: (Smith, J.) Yes. A foreign arbitral award may be confirmed by a U.S. court. The United States is a signatory to the 1958 U.N. Convention on the Recognition and Enforcement of Foreign Arbitral Awards. This Convention had the effect of permitting the courts of signatory nations to confirm and enforce foreign arbitral awards, and raised a presumption of the validity of such awards. Various exceptions exist; however, none are applicable here. Article V(2)(b) allows a court to deny enforcement if doing so will violate the public policy of the forum state. However, this exception is to be narrowly construed; only when enforcement would tend to violate the most basic notions of morality and justice will enforcement be denied; such is not the case here. Article V(2)(a) authorizes a court to deny enforcement if the subject matter is not appropriate for arbitration; however, no serious argument can be made that breach of contract is not an appropriate subject. Article V(1)(b) allows a court to deny enforcement if the opposing party was not allowed to present a fair defense. Here, an important witness for Parsons (P) declined to testify due to a speaking engagement. This is insufficient to establish a lack of due process. Article V(1)(c) permits non-enforcement if the award is rendered in excess of the arbitrator's jurisdiction. Here, the tribunal awarded certain damages which Parsons (P) contended were consequential, and prohibited by the contract. The tribunal, however, considered them to be direct, and this court will not second-guess the tribunal's construction of the contract. Finally, an implied defense against awards "in manifest violation of the law" is urged. Whether such a defense exists need not be decided; no violation has been shown here. In summation, nothing to rebut the presumption favoring enforceability has been shown, and the district court's judgment was therefore appropriate. Affirmed.

ANALYSIS

The Convention was adopted in 1958. The basic purpose was to liberalize procedures for enforcing foreign arbitral awards. Numerous procedural reforms from the previous international agreement in this area, the 1927 Geneva Convention, were made. Perhaps the most important was the shifting of the burden of proof onto the one challenging the award.

Quicknotes

ARBITRATION An agreement to have a dispute heard and decided by a neutral third party, rather than through legal proceedings.

BREACH OF CONTRACT Unlawful failure by a party to perform its obligations pursuant to contract.

DUE PROCESS CLAUSE Clauses, found in the Fifth and Fourteenth Amendments to the United States Constitution, providing that no person shall be deprived of "life, liberty, or property, without due process of law."

FORCE MAJEURE CLAUSE Clause, pursuant to an oil and gas lease, relieving the lessee from liability for breach of the lease if the party's performance is impeded as the result of a natural cause that could not have been prevented.

Note: There are no principal cases in Chapter 5 of the casebook.

CHAPTER 6

Foreign Sovereign Immunity and the Act of State Doctrine

Quick Reference Rules of Law

Verlinden B.V. v. Central Bank of Nigeria

Dutch corporation (P) v. Nigerian government (D)

461 U.S. 480 (1983).

NATURE OF CASE: Appeal of dismissal of action brought in federal court against a foreign state under the Foreign Sovereign Immunities Act.

FACT SUMMARY: **A federal circuit court held that provisions of the Foreign Sovereign Immunities Act permitting suits against foreign sovereigns by foreign nationals in federal court were unconstitutional.**

RULE OF LAW

Provisions of the Foreign Sovereign Immunities Act permitting suits against foreign sovereigns by foreign nationals in federal court are constitutional.

FACTS: Verlinden B.V. (P), a Dutch corporation, became involved in a contract dispute with the Central Bank of Nigeria (the Bank) (D), an arm of the Nigerian government. It brought suit in federal district court for breach of contract, with jurisdiction based on the 1976 Foreign Sovereign Immunities Act (Act). The Bank (D) moved to dismiss on both personal and subject matter jurisdictional grounds. The district court held the Act not to apply to the controversy at hands. The Second Circuit Court of Appeals affirmed, but on the grounds that the provisions of the Act permitting suits against foreign sovereigns by foreign nationals violated the "arising under" provisions of Article III of the U.S. Constitution. The United States Supreme Court granted review.

ISSUE: Are provisions of the Foreign Sovereign Immunities Act permitting suits against foreign sovereigns by foreign nationals in federal court constitutional?

HOLDING AND DECISION: (Burger, C.J.) Yes. Provisions of the Foreign Sovereign Immunities Act permitting suits against foreign sovereigns by foreign nationals in federal court are constitutional. Because of its Article I powers over foreign commerce and foreign relations, Congress has the power to decide as a matter of federal law whether and under what circumstances foreign nations should be amenable to suit in the United States. It is constrained in this case only by Article III's limitation on the expansion of the jurisdiction of the federal courts. In passing the Act, Congress sought to funnel cases against foreign sovereigns away from state courts and into federal courts, and the resulting jurisdiction is within the bounds of the Constitution, since a suit against a foreign state necessarily raises questions of substantive federal law, and hence clearly "arises under" federal law as that term is used in Article III. The Act also concerns the types of actions to which foreign sovereigns may be subjected to U.S. courts. This clearly is a proper function of Congress, and the Act therefore violated neither Article I nor III. Reversed and remanded.

ANALYSIS

The strict rule regarding sovereign immunity can be traced back as far as 1812, with the decision *The Schooner Exchange v. M'Faddon*, 7 Cranch 116 (1812). There, Chief Justice Marshall held foreign sovereigns absolutely immune from suit in any U.S. (or state) court. This principle was never raised to a constitutional requirement, however, and by the mid-twentieth century had been abandoned.

Quicknotes

PERSONAL JURISDICTION The court's authority over a person or parties to a law suit.

SOVEREIGN IMMUNITY Immunity of government from suit without its consent.

SUBJECT MATTER JURISDICTION A court's ability to adjudicate a specific category of cases based on the subject matter of the dispute.

Mohamed Ali Samantar v. Bashe Abdi Yousef et al.

Former prime minister of Somalia (D) v. Natives of Somalia (P)

130 S. Ct. 2278 (2010).

NATURE OF CASE: Appeal from circuit court's decision in favor of the plaintiffs.

FACT SUMMARY: The plaintiffs, including Mr. Yousef (P), are residents of Somalia who allege that Samantar (D), the former Prime Minister, authorized their torture as well as extrajudicial killings while he served as Prime Minister.

RULE OF LAW

An individual sued for conduct taken in his official capacity is not a foreign state under the meaning of the Foreign Services Immunities Act.

FACTS: The plaintiffs, including Mr. Yousef (P), are a group of well-educated and prosperous Somalis. They allege that Samantar (D), first as Minister of Defense and then as Prime Minister of Somalia, authorized their persecution and personally aided and abetted those in the Somalia military that were carrying out their torture during the 1980s. In 1991, Samantar (D) fled Somalia and is now a resident of Virginia. The plaintiffs filed their complaint in federal district court alleging violations of the Torture Victim Protection Act. Samantar (D) made a claim of sovereign immunity and the district court stayed the action after providing the State Department with the opportunity to take a position regarding Samantar's (D) alleged sovereign immune status. After the State Department made no response, the district court found that Samantar (D) was immune from suit because the Foreign Service Immunities Act extended to individual officials acting on behalf of the foreign state. The Second Circuit Court of Appeals reversed and Samantar (D) appealed to the United States Supreme Court.

ISSUE: Is an individual sued for conduct taken in his official capacity a foreign state under the meaning of the Foreign Services Immunities Act?

HOLDING AND DECISION: (Stevens, J.) No. An individual sued for conduct taken in his official capacity is not a foreign state under the meaning of the Foreign Services Immunities Act ("FSIA" or "the Act"). FSIA provides that a foreign state shall be immune from the jurisdiction of the courts of the United States and of the individual states. Samantar (D) argues that he is immune from suit because he was acting in his official capacity on behalf of a foreign state. The Act defines "foreign state" as the state itself, any political subdivision thereof, or any separate agency or legal entity acting on behalf of the state. The statute does not include foreign officials in its definition. Instead, the act refers only to legal entities acting on behalf of the state. Accordingly, referring solely to FSIA, an individual sued for conduct taken in his official capacity is not a foreign state and is not subject to immunity under the Act. However, that is not the end of the inquiry. On remand, the trial court should determine if the state is a necessary party to the action because its interests cannot be protected otherwise. Also, it may be that a suit against an individual in his official capacity is in fact a suit against the state itself, based on the real party in interest doctrine. Lastly, the former common law procedure exists for Samantar (D). Under the common law, foreign officials, as opposed to foreign states, may be immune from suit if the State Department files a suggestion of immunity with the district court. The Second Circuit's reversal is affirmed and the case is remanded to the district court. Affirmed.

ANALYSIS

Congress enacted FSIA to trump the former common law procedure for dealing with claims of immunity by foreign states. Under that procedure, the district court would inquire with the State Department whether there was a "suggestion of immunity." If the State Department filed such statement, the district court was divested of jurisdiction. Here, the Supreme Court noted that procedure still exists, in name at least, for actions against foreign individual officials.

Quicknotes

IMMUNITY Exemption from a legal obligation.

Republic of Austria v. Altmann

Foreign state (D) v. American citizen (P)

541 U.S. 677 (2004).

NATURE OF CASE: Action by American citizen against foreign state to recover personal property.

FACT SUMMARY: Altmann (P) filed suit against Austria (D) under the Foreign Sovereign Immunities Act of 1976 for the recovery of paintings seized by the Nazis or taken by Austria after World War II.

RULE OF LAW

The Foreign Sovereign Immunities Act of 1976 applies to actions that took place before its passage.

FACTS: Maria Altmann (P), the American heir of the original owner of several paintings by Gustav Klimt, learned that the artwork had been either seized by the Nazis or taken by Austria (D) after World War II. She sued Austria (D) and the state-owned Austrian Gallery (D) in American federal court, to recover the paintings confiscated by the Nazis in violation of international law. She filed the suit under the Foreign Sovereign Immunities Act of 1976 (FSIA), which allows suits against foreign nations in cases involving "rights to property taken in violation of international law." Austria (D), however, claimed that the FSIA did not apply in this case because the paintings were taken in the 1940s, when the United States embraced a different and more extensive idea of immunity that would have barred the suit. Because the Act did not explicitly state that it applied retroactively (that is, to actions taken before it was passed) Austria claimed that it was entitled to this broader definition of immunity. The district court sided with Altmann (P), holding that the FSIA applied retroactively. The Ninth Circuit Court of Appeals affirmed.

ISSUE: Does the Foreign Sovereign Immunities Act of 1976 apply to actions that took place before its passage?

HOLDING AND DECISION: (Stevens, J.) Yes. The Foreign Sovereign Immunities Act of 1976 applies to actions that took place before its passage. While the Act does not explicitly state that it should be applied to actions that took place before its passage, there are strong indications in the text of the statute that Congress intended it to apply retroactively. The language of the Act suggests Congress intended courts to resolve all immunity claims—not actions protected by immunity, but assertions of immunity to suits arising from those actions—in conformity with the principles set forth in the Act, regardless of when the underlying conduct occurred. Here, Austria's claim of immunity clearly falls within the Act's purpose. Review of the district and appeals courts declined.

CONCURRENCE: (Breyer, J.) The legal concept of sovereign immunity is a defendant's status at the time of suit, not about a defendant's conduct before the suit. In addition, there are legal principles that protect actual past reliance.

DISSENT: (Kennedy, J.) The rule against the retroactivity of statutes has been diminished by the majority. Retroactivity is a rule of fairness based on respect for expectations and should not be abruptly taken away.

ANALYSIS

This is one of the more recent cases dealing with anti-retroactivity, which is a doctrine holding that courts should not construe a statute to apply retroactively unless there is a clear statutory intent that it should.

Quicknotes

SOVEREIGN IMMUNITY Immunity of government from suit without its consent.

Saudi Arabia v. Nelson

Foreign government (D) v. Injured (P)

507 U.S. 349 (1993).

NATURE OF CASE: Appeal from a judgment for the plaintiff in a personal injury action against a sovereign government.

FACT SUMMARY: Saudi Arabia (D) claimed foreign sovereign immunity from the subject-matter jurisdiction of the federal courts after Nelson (P) filed suit against it, alleging wrongful arrest, imprisonment, and torture.

RULE OF LAW

Foreign states are entitled to immunity from the jurisdiction of courts in the United States, unless the action is based upon commercial activity in the manner of a private player within the market.

FACTS: Nelson (P) was recruited in the United States for employment as a monitoring systems engineer at a hospital in Riyadh, Saudi Arabia (D). When Nelson (P) discovered safety defects in the hospital's oxygen and nitrous oxide lines, he repeatedly advised hospital officials of the defects and reported them to a Saudi government (D) commission as well. Hospital officials instructed Nelson (P) to ignore the problems. Several months later, he was called in to the hospital's security office, arrested, and transported to a jail cell, where he was shackled, tortured, beaten, and kept without food for four days. After 39 days, the Saudi government (D) released Nelson (P), allowing him to leave the country. Nelson (P) and his wife (P) filed this action in the United States, seeking damages for personal injury. They also claimed a basis for recovery in Saudi Arabia's (D) failure to warn Nelson (P) of the hidden dangers associated with his employment. The Saudi government (D) appealed the judgment of the court of appeals.

ISSUE: Are foreign states entitled to immunity from the jurisdiction of courts in the United States, unless the action is based upon a commercial activity in the manner of a private player within the market?

HOLDING AND DECISION: (Souter, J.) Yes. Foreign states are entitled to immunity from the jurisdiction of courts in the United States, unless the action is based upon a commercial activity in the manner of a private player within the market. Saudi Arabia's (D) tortious conduct in this case fails to qualify as "commercial activity" within the meaning of the Foreign Sovereign Immunities Act of 1976. Its conduct boils down to abuse of the power of its police by the Saudi government (D). A foreign state's exercise of the power of its police is peculiarly sovereign in nature and is not the sort of activity engaged in by private parties. Furthermore, Nelson's (P) failure to warn claim must also fail; sovereign nations have no duty to warn of their propensity for tortious conduct. Nelson's (P) action is not based upon a commercial activity within the meaning of the Act and therefore is outside the subject-matter jurisdiction of the federal courts. Motion to dismiss is granted. Reversed.

CONCURRENCE: (White, J.) Neither the hospital's employment practices nor its disciplinary procedures have any apparent connection to this country. Absent a nexus to the United States, the Act does not grant Nelson's (P) access to our courts.

CONCURRENCE AND DISSENT: (Kennedy, J.) The Nelsons' (P) claims alleging negligence in failing during Nelson's (P) recruitment to warn him of foreseeable dangers are based upon commercial activity having substantial contact with the United States. As such, they are within the commercial activity exception to the Act and within the jurisdiction of the federal courts. They ought to be remanded to the district court for further consideration.

ANALYSIS

Under the "restrictive," as opposed to the "absolute," theory of foreign sovereign immunity, a state is immune from the jurisdiction of foreign courts as to its sovereign or public acts but not as to those that are private or commercial in character. A state engages in commercial activity under the restrictive theory where it exercises only those powers that can also be exercised by private citizens, as distinct from those powers peculiar to sovereigns. Whether a state acts in the manner of a private party is a question of behavior, not motivation. While it is difficult to distinguish the purpose of conduct from its nature, the Court recognized that the Act unmistakably commands it to observe the distinction.

Quicknotes

SOVEREIGN IMMUNITY Immunity of government from suit without its consent.

SUBJECT MATTER JURISDICTION A court's ability to adjudicate a specific category of cases based on the subject matter of the dispute.

Letelier v. Republic of Chile

Foreign nation's ambassador (P) v. Foreign nation (D)

488 F. Supp. 665 (D.D.C. 1980).

NATURE OF CASE: Tort causes of action under common law and international law.

FACT SUMMARY: Letelier (P), former ambassador to Chile (D), and Mofitt (P), were killed by a car bomb in the United States. Their families brought suit in the United States against Chile (D) and its officials, alleging they were responsible for the bombing. Chile (D) denied responsibility and asserted sovereign immunity.

RULE OF LAW

(1) Section 1605(a)(5) of the Foreign Sovereign Immunity Act does not require a finding that a tortious act of a foreign nation be "private" as a condition for excepting the act from sovereign immunity.

(2) For purposes of the exception from sovereign immunity provided by § 1605(a)(5) of the Foreign Sovereign Immunity Act, a decision to assassinate an individual is not a discretionary act excluded from the exception.

FACTS: Letelier (P), former ambassador to Chile (D), and Mofitt (P), were killed by a car bomb in Washington, D.C. Their families brought several tortious causes of action in the United States under international law, the common law, the Constitution, and legislative enactments against Chile (D), its intelligence agency, and various Chilean officials, alleging they were responsible for the bombing. Chile (D) denied responsibility and asserted sovereign immunity. The families asserted under § 1605(a)(5) of the Foreign Sovereign Immunity Act that Chile (D) did not have the claimed immunity. That section exempts from immunity a money damages action for wrongful death that occurs in the United States and that is caused by the tortious action of a foreign state or its officials or employees while acting within the scope of their office or employment. The section has two exclusions. The first, subsection (A), excludes any claim "based upon the exercise or performance or the failure to exercise or perform a discretionary function regardless of whether the discretion be abused." The second, subsection (B), excludes claims that arise "out of malicious prosecution, abuse of process, libel, slander, misrepresentation, deceit, or interference with contract rights." However, neither of these exclusions was invoked by Chile (D).

ISSUE:

(1) Does § 1605(a)(5) of the Foreign Sovereign Immunity Act require a finding that a tortious act of a foreign nation be "private" as a condition for excepting the act from sovereign immunity?

(2) For purposes of the exception from sovereign immunity provided by § 1 605(a)(5) of the Foreign Sovereign Immunity Act, is a decision to assassinate an individual a discretionary act excluded from the exception?

HOLDING AND DECISION: (Green, J.)

(1) No. Section 1605(a)(5) of the Foreign Sovereign Immunity Act (the Act) does not require a finding that a tortious act of a foreign nation be "private" as a condition for excepting the act from sovereign immunity. Chile's (D) argument that the intent of Congress was to include only private torts like automobile accidents in the section's exclusion from immunity, and that political assassinations are public in nature, ignores the plain meaning of the section. The Act does not limit its application to tortious acts that are private only. Along with the words of the section itself, the other provisions of the Act clearly indicate an intent that the Act apply to all claims of sovereign immunity. The legislative history also does not support Chile's (D) assertion because, although automobile accidents were a prime concern of Congress, Congress made it clear that the Act applies to all tortious actions for money damages, so as to provide compensation for traffic accidents or other noncommercial torts.

(2) No. For purposes of the exception from sovereign immunity provided by § 1605(a)(5) of the Foreign Sovereign Immunity Act, a decision to assassinate an individual is not a discretionary act excluded from the exception. Here, too, the exclusions in § 1605(a)(5)(A) and (B) are inapplicable. The claims here did not arise from any of the specific causes of action enumerated in (B). As for the exclusion found in (A) for discretionary acts, although a decision calculated to result in injury or death to a particular individual involves discretion, it has been recognized that there is no discretion to commit an illegal act. Therefore, § 1605(a)(5)(A) also does not apply. For these reasons, Chile (D) cannot claim sovereign immunity.

ANALYSIS

Some courts have held that for purposes of § 1605(a)(5) the tortious act or omission, in addition to the injury, must occur in the United States. Others, as well as the Restatement (Third) of the Foreign Relations Law of the United

Continued on next page.

States, however, have construed the noncommercial tort exception as applying whenever the injury occurs in the United States, regardless of where the act or omission causing the injury occurred.

Quicknotes

SOVEREIGN IMMUNITY Immunity of government from suit without its consent.

Risk v. Halvorsen

U.S. citizen (P) v. Foreign government officials (D)

936 F.2d 393 (9th Cir. 1991).

NATURE OF CASE: Appeal from decision rejecting jurisdiction over a foreign nation under § 1605(a)(5) of the Foreign Sovereign Immunity Act.

FACT SUMMARY: Elisabeth Risk (Elisabeth), a Norwegian citizen, was under court order to not leave the United States with her children. Norwegian government officials (D) helped Elisabeth to leave the country in violation of the court order, and the children's father, Larry Risk (Larry) (P), sued the Norwegian government (D). The Norwegian government (D) claimed sovereign immunity.

RULE OF LAW

For purposes of the exception from sovereign immunity provided by § 1605(a)(5) of the Foreign Sovereign Immunity Act, a decision by a foreign nation to assist its citizens and the citizens' children to leave the United States in violation of a U.S. court order is a discretionary act excluded from the exception.

FACTS: Larry Risk (Larry) (P), a U.S. citizen, married Elisabeth Risk (Elisabeth), a native and citizen of Norway. They had two children, and, after the family moved to Norway, Larry (P) violated a temporary Norwegian County Court order providing him with ordinary visitation rights when he returned to the United States with the children during the first visitation period. Subsequently, the Superior Court of San Francisco awarded Larry and Elisabeth joint custody of their children, and prohibited the parents from removing the children from the San Francisco area. They were also required to surrender their passports, and were prohibited from applying for replacement passports without a court order. Nonetheless, with the assistance of Norwegian government officials (D), Elisabeth returned to Norway with the children. Larry (P) filed suit, alleging that the Norwegian government (D) and its officials (D) violated the custody order by providing Elisabeth with travel documentation, financial aid and advice, and by obstructing Larry's (P) efforts in finding his children. The district court ruled that it had no jurisdiction over Norway under Foreign Sovereign Immunity Act because of an exception in § 1605(a)(5), which excludes claims based on discretionary function. The court of appeals granted review.

ISSUE: For purposes of the exception from sovereign immunity provided by § 1605(a)(5) of the Foreign Sovereign Immunity Act, is a decision by a foreign nation to assist its citizen and the citizen's children to leave the United States in violation of a U.S. court order a discretionary act excluded from the exception?

HOLDING AND DECISION: (Brunetti, J.) Yes. For purposes of the exception from sovereign immunity provided by § 1605(a)(5) of the Foreign Sovereign Immunity Act (FSIA), a decision by a foreign nation to assist its citizen and the citizen's children to leave the United States in violation of a U.S. court order is a discretionary act excluded from the exception. Whether the Norwegian government officials (D) are within the discretionary function exception to the FSIA depends first on whether the officials had any discretion to act or if there was an element of choice as to conduct, and, second, whether the decisions were grounded in social, economic, and political policy. Here, there can be no doubt that the Norwegian officials (D) were exercising discretion. Larry (P) argues that because the officials' (D) acts may constitute a violation of California criminal law, the acts should fall outside the scope of the discretionary function exception. This argument is rejected because, although some acts that are clearly contrary to the precepts of humanity (such as assassination) are deemed to have no discretionary element, it cannot be said that every conceivably illegal act is outside the scope of the discretionary function exception. Affirmed.

ANALYSIS

The court noted that determining whether an act is discretionary is controlled by principles developed under the Federal Tort Claims Act (FTCA). This is because the FSIA's discretionary function limitation was modeled on a similar provision in the FTCA. Consequently, when applying the FSIA's discretionary function provision, courts have looked to decisions from the FTCA area. The Supreme Court has held that the FTCA's discretionary function limitation does not apply when a federal statute, regulation, or policy specifically prescribes a course of action for a government official or employee. Lower courts have interpreted that to mean that prohibited conduct does not fall within the FTCA's discretionary function limitation. Arguably, then, conduct that is proscribed in a foreign nation should also not fall within the FSIA's discretionary function limitation.

Quicknotes

JURISDICTION The authority of a court to hear and declare judgment in respect to a particular matter.

SOVEREIGN IMMUNITY Immunity of government from suit without its consent.

Murphy v. Islamic Republic of Iran

Families of slain U.S. soldiers (P) v. Foreign country (D)

740 F. Supp. 2d 51 (D.D.C. 2010).

NATURE OF CASE: Consideration by federal trial court of plaintiffs' motion to take advantage of new changes to the Foreign Sovereign Immunities Act.

FACT SUMMARY: In 1983, the terrorist organization Hezbollah, with the assistance of Iran, carried out the bombing and murder of 241 United States Marines in Beirut, Lebanon.

RULE OF LAW

For a court to have subject matter jurisdiction over a foreign state, the case must satisfy four elements of the Foreign Services Immunities Act: a statutory grant of original jurisdiction, waiver of sovereign immunity, the requirement that an actual claim be heard, and the claim must be filed within the ten year statute of limitations.

FACTS: In 1983, the terrorist organization Hezbollah, with the assistance of Iran, carried out the bombing and murder of 241 U.S. Marines in Beirut, Lebanon. The plaintiffs in this case are made up of the estates of slain U.S. soldiers and their family members. The defendants are the Islamic Republic of Iran (D) and its Ministry of Information and Security (MOIS) (D). This court takes judicial notice of the determination of *Peterson v. Islamic Republic of Iran*, 515 F. Supp. 2d 25 (D.D.C. 2007), where the liability of Iran (D) and MOIS (D) for the Beirut bombing was conclusively established. The plaintiffs filed this action against the same defendants to take advantage of the 2008 statutory changes to the Foreign Services Immunities Act (FSIA). The new changes provide a federal cause of action for the plaintiffs and also allow punitive damages. The plaintiffs seek to take advantage of these modifications retroactively. The court must examine the complaint to determine if it meets all of the pleading requirements of the new section of FSIA, 1605A.

ISSUE: For a court to have subject matter jurisdiction over a foreign state, must the case satisfy four elements of the Foreign Services Immunities Act: a statutory grant of original jurisdiction, waiver of sovereign immunity, the requirement that an actual claim be heard, and the claim must be filed within the ten year statute of limitations?

HOLDING AND DECISION: (Lamberth, C.J.) Yes. For a court to have subject matter jurisdiction over a foreign state, the case must satisfy four elements of the Foreign Services Immunities Act (FSIA): a statutory grant of original jurisdiction, waiver of sovereign immunity, the requirement that an actual claim be heard, and the claim must be filed within the 10-year statute of limitations. First, FSIA grants district courts original jurisdiction to hear civil cases against foreign states. Because this case is against Iran (D) and one of its instrumentalities, that element is satisfied. Second, there must be a waiver of sovereign immunity. Under FSIA, that immunity is waived when a foreign state commits an act of torture or extrajudicial killing which caused personal injury or death. The plaintiffs' complaint pleads all of those elements and therefore Iran (D) is not entitled to immunity. Third, a court will "hear a claim" under FSIA when certain conditions are met. The foreign state must be designated by the State Department as a state sponsor of terrorism. The claimant must be a U.S. national, member of the armed forces, or a contracted individual doing work on behalf of the United States. Lastly, when the complained of act occurred in the foreign state, the claimant must afford the foreign state a reasonable opportunity to arbitrate the claim in accordance with international rules of arbitration. The plaintiffs have satisfied each of those factors. The arbitration factor is inapplicable because the complained of act occurred in Lebanon and not Iran. The fourth factor under the subject matter jurisdiction analysis, the limitations period, is also satisfied. As to other issues beyond subject matter jurisdiction, the court has personal jurisdiction over the defendants in accordance with Section 1608. The Fifth Amendment's minimum contacts rules do not apply. As to liability and damages, there is no question Iran (D) and MOIS (D) are liable for providing material support to Hezbollah for carrying out the bombing. The plaintiffs will be entitled to damages for pain and suffering, economic losses, and possible punitive damages.

ANALYSIS

Because Iran (D) did not respond to the case, the district court entered a default judgment against it. The plaintiffs now must proceed through the State Department and its diplomatic channels to serve the default judgment upon Iran (D). Resolution of the matter will be handled by the State Department.

Quicknotes

SOVEREIGN IMMUNITY Immunity of government from suit without its consent.

SUBJECT MATTER JURISDICTION The authority of the court to hear and decide actions involving a particular type of issue or subject.

United States v. Noriega

Federal government (P) v. Foreign general (D)

117 F.3d 1206 (11th Cir. 1997).

NATURE OF CASE: Appeal of indictment and prosecution of a foreign leader for alleged narcotics offenses.

FACT SUMMARY: Because Noriega (D) was believed to be trafficking in narcotics solely for his own personal benefit, he was forcefully brought to the United States (P) to face criminal charges for those activities.

RULE OF LAW

A head of state is not subject to the jurisdiction of foreign courts for official acts taken during the ruler's term of office.

FACTS: After General Noriega (D) was forcefully brought to this country to face criminal charges, he was indicted and prosecuted for allegedly trafficking in narcotics solely for his own personal benefit. Noriega's (D) counsel moved to dismiss the indictment on the ground that United States (P) laws could not be applied to a foreign leader whose alleged illegal activities all occurred outside the territorial bounds of the United States (P). His counsel further argued that Noriega (D) was immune from prosecution as a head of state and diplomat, and that his alleged narcotics offenses constituted acts of state not properly reviewable by this court. A jury found Noriega guilty of eight counts in the indictment and not guilty of the remaining two counts. Noriega (D) was convicted and sentenced to consecutive prison terms of 20, 15, and 5 years.

ISSUE: Is a head of state subject to the jurisdiction of foreign courts for official acts taken during the ruler's term of office?

HOLDING AND DECISION: (Kravitch, J.) No. A head of state is not subject to the jurisdiction of foreign courts for official acts taken during the ruler's term of office. Officially, Noriega (D) is the Commandante of the Panamanian Defense Forces. However, he was never elected to head Panama's government. More important, the United States (P) government has never accorded Noriega (D) head-of-state status. The executive branch's decision to recognize President Delvalle and not Noriega (D) as Panama's head of state is binding on the court. Simply because Noriega (D) may have run the country of Panama does not mean he is entitled to head-of-state immunity. Moreover, criminal activities such as the narcotics trafficking with which Noriega (D) is charged can hardly be considered official acts or governmental duties that promote a sovereign state's interests, especially where, as here, the activity was allegedly undertaken solely for the personal benefit of the foreign leader. Since the United States (P) has never recognized Noriega (D) as Panama's head of state, he has no claim to head-of-state immunity. Affirmed.

ANALYSIS

Immunity for Special Missions is found in Article 25 of the United Nations Convention on Special Missions, which entered into force in June of 1985. The court here declared that accepting Noriega's (D) contention that he must be granted immunity from prosecution regardless of his source of power or nature of rule would allow illegitimate dictators the benefit of their unscrupulous and possibly brutal seizures of power. No authority exists for such a novel extension of head-of-state immunity, and the court declined to create one here.

Quicknotes

IMMUNITY Exemption from a legal obligation.

JURISDICTION The authority of a court to hear and declare judgment in respect to a particular matter.

Banco Nacional de Cuba v. Sabbatino, Receiver

Cuban government (P) v. Receiver (D)

376 U.S. 398 (1964).

NATURE OF CASE: Review of order dismissing action for damages for breach of contract.

FACT SUMMARY: Faced with a breach of contract action by the Cuban government (P), Sabbatino (D) contended that an earlier expropriation of property, not protected by the act of state doctrine, constituted an offset.

RULE OF LAW

The act of state doctrine is available to a foreign government plaintiff which has expropriated property of the party it sues.

FACTS: In 1960, the Castro government of Cuba (P) nationalized certain U.S.-owned companies. One such company was Compania Azucarera, a sugar distributor. Azucarera had contracted to sell sugar to Farr, Whitlock & Co. After the sugar was nationalized, Farr, Whitlock entered into another contract, this time with the Cuban government (P). The sugar was delivered, but Farr, Whitlock refused to pay the Cuban government (P), but rather turned the proceeds over to Sabbatino (D), a receiver appointed for Azucarera's assets. The Cuban government (P) brought a breach of contract action. Sabbatino (D) raised the expropriation as an offset. The district court, rejecting the Cuban government's (P) act of state defense, granted summary judgment in favor of Sabbatino (D). The court of appeals affirmed, and the United States Supreme Court granted review.

ISSUE: Is the act of state doctrine available to a foreign government plaintiff which has expropriated the property of the party it sues?

HOLDING AND DECISION: (Harlan, J.) Yes. The act of state doctrine is available to a foreign government plaintiff which has expropriated property of the party it sues. As long ago as the last century, this Court recognized that U.S. courts may not sit in judgment of the propriety of acts done by a government within its borders. This has consistently been reaffirmed ever since. However, several reasons are advanced for not applying the act of state doctrine to a foreign government plaintiff which has expropriated property of the defendant, in this case Sabbatino's (D) predecessor. The first is that the doctrine should not apply to acts violating international law. This is incorrect. The act of state doctrine does not arise from international law; traditionally, it has been a matter of comity between individual nations. No international agreements recognize it. The other argument is that the executive must approve its application in any specific case for it to be binding on federal courts. This is a simplistic view of the role of the judiciary in this area. The judiciary's interest in rendering decisions involving foreign bodies becomes greater in matters of consensus of codification; the less consensual or codified a concept is, the more the matter should be left to political branches of government. The matter of expropriation of foreign assets by a nation is a highly controversial one, an issue hardly near consensus in the international community. Consequently, it is a matter best left for the political branches to address. An expropriation therefore should not be the subject of judgment by a U.S. court, being a nonjusticiable act of state. Here, the basis for allowing the offset was the district court's conclusion that it could adjudicate the Venezuelan government's expropriation, and this was erroneous. Reversed and remanded.

DISSENT: (White, J.) The Court has declared the application of international law beyond the competence of U.S. courts in an important category of cases. The Court is incorrect in its assertion that the act of state doctrine cannot be adjudicated by reference to international law.

ANALYSIS

The present decision was not popular in the political branches of government, particularly Congress. Not long after the decision was rendered, Congress enacted 22 U.S.C. § 2370(e)(2), a statutory overruling of the instant case. While the law has survived constitutional attack, courts tend to construe it narrowly.

Quicknotes

ACT OF STATE DOCTRINE Prohibits United States courts from investigating acts of other countries committed within their borders.

NONJUSTICIABLE Matter which is inappropriate for judicial review.

W.S. Kirkpatrick & Co. v. Environmental Tectonics Corp.

Contractor (D) v. Competitor (P)

493 U.S. 400 (1990).

NATURE OF CASE: Review of order reversing dismissal of action for damages for violation of federal statute.

FACT SUMMARY: An action involving alleged bribes to foreign officials was dismissed as nonjusticiable under the act of state doctrine.

RULE OF LAW

An action involving alleged bribes to foreign officials will not be nonjusticiable under the Act of State Doctrine.

FACTS: A principal of W.S. Kirkpatrick & Co. (D) was alleged to have effected certain bribes of Nigerian officials to secure a government contract, in violation of the federal Foreign Corrupt Practices Act and Nigerian law. Environmental Tectonics Corp. (P), a competitor for the contract, filed an action seeking damages under the federal RICO law. The district court dismissed the action, holding that since the suit implicated the actions of Nigerian officials, the act of state doctrine applied. The Third Circuit Court of Appeals reversed, and the United States Supreme Court granted review.

ISSUE: Will an action involving alleged bribes to foreign officials be nonjusticiable under the act of state doctrine?

HOLDING AND DECISION: (Scalia, J.) No. An action involving alleged bribes to foreign officials will not be nonjusticiable under the act of state doctrine. The Act of State Doctrine has been described as a consequence of domestic separation of powers; to wit, a recognition by the judiciary that certain situations involving relations with foreign governments are a matter of concern for the executive, and judicial decisions respecting such issues could interfere with executive action in this area. Essentially it is for the executive to engage in foreign affairs and to pass on the validity of foreign acts of state. When these concerns are not implicated, the act of state doctrine is not applicable. When a judicial decision does not pass on such validity, no reason for abstaining from otherwise proper jurisdiction exists. In this particular case, no issue exists as to the validity of any act by the Nigerian government. The issues pertain to the alleged actions by agents of W.S. Kirkpatrick (D). Since the outcome of the present case only tangentially implicates the acts of a foreign government, the Act of State Doctrine is inapplicable. Affirmed.

ANALYSIS

Over the years, the act of state doctrine has taken on an increasingly domestic focus. As late as 1918, in *Oetjen v. Central Leather Co.*, 246 U.S. 297 (1918), the Court gave as authority for the doctrine concerns of international comity. In the present action, however, the Court makes it clear that the main focus of the doctrine is intra-governmental relations, not international relations.

Quicknotes

ACT OF STATE DOCTRINE Prohibits United States courts from investigating acts of other countries committed within their borders.

NONJUSTICIABLE Matter which is inappropriate for judicial review.

RICO Racketeer Influenced and Corrupt Organization laws; federal and state statutes enacted for the purpose of prosecuting organized crime.

SEPARATION OF POWERS The system of checks and balances preventing one branch of government from infringing upon exercising the powers of another branch of government.

CHAPTER 7

Allocation of Legal Authority Among States

Quick Reference Rules of Law

Morrison v. National Australian Bank

Shareholders (P) v. Bank (D)

130 S. Ct. 2869 (2010).

NATURE OF CASE: Appeal from circuit court's affirming dismissal of complaint.

FACT SUMMARY: A group of foreign shareholders of National Australian Bank (D) sued the Bank (D) and an American mortgage company for alleged misconduct regarding securities traded on foreign exchanges.

RULE OF LAW

Section 10(b) of the Securities and Exchange Act of 1934 only applies to the purchase or sale of a security in the United States or of a security listed on an American stock exchange.

FACTS: The plaintiffs are a group of foreign born shareholders of the National Australian Bank (the Bank) (D). In 1998, the Bank (D) purchased codefendant Homeside Lending, Inc. (Homeside) (D), a mortgage company based in Florida. The transaction occurred in Australia. In 2001, the Bank (D) was forced to write down the value of Homeside (D) by over 1.75 billion dollars. The Bank's shareholders (P) allege Homeside (D) had improperly manipulated its financial models to make the company more valuable than it actually was. The complaint alleges the Bank (D) and its executives were aware of this, but did nothing to resolve the problem. The shareholders (D) brought suit against the Bank (D) and Homeside (D) for violations of Section 10(b) of the Securities and Exchange Act of 1934 in U.S. District Court in New York. The District Court dismissed the action for lack of subject matter jurisdiction and the Second Circuit Court of Appeals affirmed. The shareholders (P) appealed to the United States Supreme Court.

ISSUE: Does Section 10(b) of the Securities and Exchange Act of 1934 only apply to the purchase or sale of a security in the United States or of a security listed on an American stock exchange?

HOLDING AND DECISION: (Scalia, J.) Yes. Section 10(b) of the Securities and Exchange Act of 1934 only applies to the purchase or sale of a security in the United States or of a security listed on an American stock exchange. Congressional legislation only applies to the territorial jurisdiction of the United States. To give a particular statute extraterritorial effect, Congress must clearly express such intention. Where a statute is silent on the issue, it shall only apply domestically. The shareholders (P) argue that Section 10(b) has several references regarding foreign commerce that reflect Congress's intention that the statute apply beyond the jurisdiction of the United States. General references in the statute to foreign commerce do not constitute a clear expression of extraterritorial effect. In addition, while Homeside (D) is a Florida company and that is where the manipulative conduct occurred, Section 10(b) does not apply to conduct. Instead, it applies to the purchase or sale of securities. It is the financial transactions that are the focus of Section 10(b). Here, all aspects of the purchase of Homeside (D) occurred outside of the United States and also did not involve any security that is traded on an American stock exchange. Therefore, dismissal is proper because the shareholders (P) have failed to state a claim upon which relief may be granted. Affirmed.

CONCURRENCE: (Stevens, J.) While dismissal of the complaint is proper in this case, the majority improperly did away with four decades of jurisprudence regarding the general approach regarding the reach of Section 10(b). The prior rule, established by Judge Friendly of the Second Circuit Court of Appeals, used a conduct and effects test. That test examined whether the alleged wrongful conduct occurred in the United States and whether that conduct had an effect in the United States or upon citizens of the United States. No one in this litigation disputes Section 10(b) should not apply to entirely foreign transactions; however, it should apply to some transnational securities fraud cases where the wrongful conduct occurred in the United States. In this case, it was the actions of the Australian Bank executives that are at issue, and accordingly, even under the conduct and effects test, the case should be dismissed for failure to state a claim.

ANALYSIS

By jettisoning the well-established conduct and effects test, this decision has drawn widespread attention. Recent decisions handed down after *Morrison* have attempted to limit its holding. Courts have noted that *Morrison* dealt with Australian shareholders suing an Australian company that traded on the Australian stock exchange. In addition, Congress is exploring its options to extend Section 10(b)'s reach to those extraterritorial securities transactions that involve wrongful conduct with a substantial effect in the United States.

Quicknotes

SECURITIES EXCHANGE ACT § 10(b) Prohibits the use of any "manipulative or deceptive device or contrivance" in connection with the purchase or sale of a security and in violation of any regulation adopted by the Securities and Exchange Commission.

Hartford Fire Insurance Co. v. California

Insurance company (D) v. State (P)

509 U.S. 764 (1993).

NATURE OF CASE: Appeal from a judgment as to jurisdiction and application of domestic law to a foreign company in a federal antitrust action.

FACT SUMMARY: Claiming that Hartford Fire Insurance Co. (Hartford) (D) and other London-based reinsurers (D) had allegedly engaged in unlawful conspiracies to affect the market for insurance in the United States, California (P) instituted an action against Hartford (D), under the Sherman Act, which the reinsurers (D) sought to dismiss under the principle of international comity.

RULE OF LAW

Where a person subject to regulation by two states can comply with the laws of both, jurisdiction may be exercised over foreign conduct since no conflict exists.

FACTS: California (P) brought an action against Hartford Fire Insurance Co. (Hartford) (D) and other London-based reinsurers (D) alleging that they had engaged in unlawful conspiracies to affect the market for insurance in the United States and that their conduct in fact produced substantial effect, thus violating the Sherman Act. Hartford (D) argued that the district court should have declined to exercise jurisdiction under the principle of international comity. The court of appeals agreed that courts should look to that principle in deciding whether to exercise jurisdiction under the Sherman Act but that other factors, including Hartford's (D) express purpose to affect U.S. commerce and the substantial nature of the effect produced, outweighed the supposed conflict, requiring the exercise of jurisdiction in this case. Hartford (D) appealed.

ISSUE: Where a person subject to regulation by two states can comply with the laws of both, may jurisdiction be exercised over foreign conduct since no conflict exists?

HOLDING AND DECISION: (Souter, J.) Yes. Where a person subject to regulation by two states can comply with the laws of both, jurisdiction may be exercised over foreign conduct since no conflict exists. The Sherman Act applies to foreign conduct that was meant to produce and does in fact produce some substantial effect in the United States. Even assuming that a court may decline to exercise Sherman Act jurisdiction over foreign conduct, international comity would not prevent a U.S. court from exercising jurisdiction in the circumstances alleged here. Since Hartford (D) does not argue that British law requires it to act in some fashion prohibited by the law of the United States or claim that its compliance with the laws of both countries is otherwise impossible, there is no conflict with British law. Since there is no irreconcilable conflict between domestic and British law, the reinsurers (D) may not invoke comity. Affirmed.

DISSENT: (Scalia, J.) The district court had subject-matter jurisdiction over the Sherman Act claims, and the Sherman Act applies to foreign nations, despite the presumption against such an application. But, even so, statutes should not be interpreted to regulate foreign persons or conduct if that regulation would conflict with principles of international law. The activity at issue here took place primarily in the United Kingdom, and Hartford (D) and the other reinsurers (D) are British subjects having their principal place of business or residence outside the United States. Great Britain regulates the London reinsurance markets and clearly has a heavy interest in regulating the activity. Finally, § 2(b) of the McCarran-Ferguson Act allows state regulatory statutes to override the Sherman Act in the insurance field in most cases, which suggests that the importance of regulation to the United States is slight.

ANALYSIS

Black's Law Dictionary, page 242 (5th ed. 1979), defines comity of nations as "[t]he recognition which one nation allows within its territory to the legislative, executive, or judicial acts of another nation, having due regard both to international duty and convenience and to the rights of its own citizens or of other persons who are under the protection of its laws." When it enacted the Foreign Trade Antitrust Improvements Act of 1982 (FTAIA), Congress expressed no view on the question of whether a court with Sherman Act jurisdiction should ever decline to exercise such jurisdiction on grounds of international comity, an issue that the Court declined to address in this case. Justice Scalia endorsed the approach of the Restatement (Third) of Foreign Relations Law, advocating that a nation having some basis for jurisdiction should nonetheless refrain from exercising that jurisdiction when the exercise of such jurisdiction is unreasonable.

Quicknotes

ANTITRUST Body of federal law prohibiting business conduct that constitutes a restraint on trade.

Continued on next page.

COMITY A rule pursuant to which courts in one state give deference to the statutes and judicial decisions of another.

SHERMAN ACT Makes every contract or conspiracy in unreasonable restraint of commerce illegal.

SUBJECT MATTER JURISDICTION A court's ability to adjudicate a specific category of cases based on the subject matter of the dispute.

F. Hoffmann-La Roche Ltd. v. Empagran S.A.

Foreign and domestic vitamin manufacturers (D) v.
Foreign and domestic vitamin distributors (P)

542 U.S. 155 (2004).

NATURE OF CASE: Appeal of federal appeals court judgment for plaintiffs.

FACT SUMMARY: Several foreign and domestic companies that purchase and resell vitamins (P) sued several foreign and domestic vitamin manufacturers (D) for illegally acting in concert to raise prices, both within the United States and in foreign countries. The district court ruled in favor of the manufacturers (D) and the appeals court reversed.

RULE OF LAW

Under the Foreign Trade Antitrust Improvements Act of 1982, Sherman Act claims do not apply to the effects of foreign price-fixing schemes if those schemes do not have domestic effects.

FACTS: The Foreign Trade Antitrust Improvements Act of 1982 (FTAIA), provides that the Sherman Act (which regulates corporate attempts to unfairly raise prices) applies to foreign commerce only if that commerce significantly harms U.S. commerce. In this case, several foreign and domestic companies that purchase and resell vitamins (P) sued several foreign and domestic vitamin manufacturers (D) for illegally acting in concert to raise prices, both within the United States and in foreign countries. The manufacturers (D) asked the district court judge to dismiss from the case those vitamin purchasers (P) that only did business in other countries. The manufacturers (D) argued that because they only did business in other countries, they could not bring claims under the Sherman Act. In response, the purchasers (P) argued that there was a link between the foreign price-fixing attempts and the domestic attempts, and could therefore be heard under the exception to the FTAIA. The district court ruled in favor of the manufacturers (D). Even though it found that the price-fixing schemes were independent of each other, the D.C. Circuit Court of Appeals reversed, holding that Congress's intent had been to prevent price-fixing both at home and abroad, and that even the foreign claims could therefore be brought under the exception to the FTAIA.

ISSUE: Under the Foreign Trade Antitrust Improvements Act of 1982, do Sherman Act claims apply to the effects of foreign price-fixing schemes if those schemes do not have domestic effects?

HOLDING AND DECISION: (Breyer, J.) No. Under the Foreign Trade Antitrust Improvements Act of 1982, Sherman Act claims do not apply to the effects of foreign price-fixing schemes if those schemes do not have domestic effects. Congress's intent in passing the FTAIA was to prevent American courts from interfering in foreign commerce. Congress made an exception for foreign commerce that affected domestic commerce, but the exception is not a general prohibition against price-fixing in all parts of the world. Reversed.

CONCURRENCE: (Scalia, J.) The majority's interpretation of the statute is correct, and is the only interpretation that is consistent with the principle that statutes should be read with deference to the application of foreign laws in their own countries.

ANALYSIS

The Sherman Act applies to foreign conduct that has substantial effects on United States commerce. This case concerns the degree to which a 1982 amendment to the Sherman Act, the Foreign Trade Antitrust Improvements Act, broadened the law's coverage. Before the Supreme Court issued its decision, the Bush administration weighed in on the issue, stating its position that the appeals court ignored the law's focus on the domestic effects of anticompetitive conduct. The administration had argued to the appeals court that the 1982 amendment extended the Sherman Act's jurisdiction only to domestic or foreign plaintiffs who can claim injury from the domestic effects of an antitrust conspiracy.

Quicknotes

ANTITRUST Body of federal law prohibiting business conduct that constitutes a restraint on trade.

SHERMAN ACT Prohibits unreasonable restraint of trade.

The Netherlands: District Court at the Hague Judgment in Compagnie Européenne des Pétroles S.A. v. Sensor Nederland B.V.

Foreign corporation (P) v. Foreign subsidiary of U.S. corporation

22 Intl. Legal Materials 66 (1983).

NATURE OF CASE: Action for breach of contract.

FACT SUMMARY: Compagnie Européenne des Pétroles S.A. (C.E.P.) (P), a French corporation, had a confirmed purchase order with Sensor Nederland B.V. (Sensor) (D), a Dutch subsidiary of a U.S. corporation, for delivery of geophones, the ultimate destination of which was the U.S.S.R. Sensor (D) claimed that as a subsidiary of an American corporation, it was subject to an export embargo that was imposed by the President of the United States during the time that revised purchase orders and confirmations were being exchanged. C.E.P. (P) sought timely performance or damages for failure to perform.

RULE OF LAW

A U.S. law that imposes export restrictions on a foreign corporation that is wholly owned by a U.S. corporation and that concludes contracts outside the United States with non-American corporations does not have extra-territorial effect under international law.

FACTS: In May 1982, Compagnie Européenne des Pétroles S.A. (C.E.P.) (P), a French corporation, placed an order for 2,400 strings of geophones with Sensor Nederland B.V. (Sensor) (D), a Dutch subsidiary of a Dutch corporation owned entirely by a U.S. corporation. The geophones were to be delivered FOB the Netherlands, by September 20, 1982, with the ultimate destination being the U.S.S.R. Subsequent revisions and confirmations occurred, and on July 1, 1982, Sensor (D) confirmed receipt of C.E.P.'s (P) final revised order. Then, on July 27, 1982, Sensor (D) claimed that as a subsidiary of an American corporation, it was subject to an export embargo that was imposed by the President of the United States on June 22, 1982. C.E.P. (P) sought timely performance by October 18, 1982, or damages for each day thereafter that Sensor (D) failed to deliver the strings of geophones. Sensor (D) defended by claiming that the sanctions for violating the embargo constituted *force majeure* and justified reliance on the exonerating circumstances provision of the Uniform Act governing the International Sale of Goods.

ISSUE: Does a U.S. law that imposes export restrictions on a foreign corporation that is wholly owned by a U.S. corporation and that concludes contracts outside the United States with non-American corporations have extra-territorial effect under international law?

HOLDING AND DECISION: [Judge not stated in casebook excerpt.] No. A U.S. law that imposes export restrictions on a foreign corporation that is wholly owned by a U.S. corporation and that concludes contracts outside the United States with non-American corporations does not have extra-territorial effect under international law. First, because the parties failed to make a choice of law, the contract is governed by the law of the Netherlands, the country where the party who is to perform has its principal place of business. Because Netherlands law is applicable, the Uniform Act governing the International Sale of Goods is also applicable. The U.S. Export Administration Regulations that purport to govern the contract between C.E.P. (P) and Sensor (D) would do so through an extra-territorial jurisdiction rule found in § 385.2(c)(2) of those Regulations. That rule is intended to apply to corporations located outside the United States that conclude contracts outside the United States with non-American corporations. Under international law, Sensor (D) has Netherlands nationality. This interpretation is supported by a Treaty of Friendship, Commerce and Navigation between the Netherlands and the United States. The issue is, therefore, whether the extra-territorial jurisdiction rule of § 385.2(c)(2) is compatible with international law. The general rule is that a State cannot exercise jurisdiction over acts performed outside its borders. Two exceptions to this general rule are the "nationality principle" and the "protection principle." The nationality principle is not operative here to the extent the U.S. jurisdiction rule covers companies of non-U.S. nationality. The protection principle also does not help Sensor (D) here. That principle states that it is permissible for a State to exercise jurisdiction over acts, regardless where or by whom they are performed, that jeopardize its security or other State interests. Such other State interests do not include the foreign policy interests that the U.S. export regulations seek to protect. Accordingly, the protection principle cannot be invoked here. Moreover, the exportation acts that the export regulations attempt to cover—the export to Russia of goods not originating in the United States by a non-American exporter—do not have any direct or illicit effects within the United States itself. Thus, for these reasons, the jurisdiction rule cannot be brought into compatibility with international law. The claim is therefore allowed, and Sensor (D) is ordered to pay costs.

ANALYSIS

The court noted that under international law there would be some instances where the extra-territorial jurisdiction

Continued on next page.

rule of the U.S. export regulations would be given effect, as where U.S. citizens set up a non-U.S. corporation outside the United States to evade a U.S. embargo. The court was quick to point out, however, that there was no evidence that had occurred in this case.

Quicknotes

F.O.B. Free on board; agreement between a seller and buyer pursuant to which the seller agrees to deliver the subject matter of the contract to a particular destination at his own expense and until which time he assumes all liability therefor.

United States v. Romero-Galue

Federal government (P) v. Ship owner (D)

757 F.2d 1147 (11th Cir. 1985).

NATURE OF CASE: Appeal of dismissal of criminal prosecution for narcotics smuggling.

FACT SUMMARY: Romero-Galue (D) was charged with violation of U.S. narcotics laws after U.S. Customs boarded his ship, of Panamanian registry, on the high seas.

RULE OF LAW

U.S. criminal laws as they apply to narcotics smuggling on the high seas may be enforced against foreign nationals.

FACTS: The "El Don" was a Panamanian ship. Observing what it considered to be suspicious activities on the high seas, U.S. Coast Guard boarded the ship and found over four tons of marijuana. Various crew members were charged with violating 21 U.S.C. § 955a(c), which imposed criminal penalties on the possession with intent to distribute narcotics on any vessel within customs waters of the United States (P). The United States (P) and Panama had a treaty permitting U.S. inspection of Panamanian ships on the high seas. The district court dismissed the indictment on the grounds that § 955a(c) did not provide jurisdiction over foreign ships on the high seas. The United States (P) appealed.

ISSUE: May U.S. criminal laws as they apply to narcotics smuggling on the high seas be enforced against foreign nationals?

HOLDING AND DECISION: (Tjoflat, J.) Yes. U.S. criminal laws as they apply to narcotics smuggling on the high seas may be enforced against foreign nationals. Under § 955a(c), jurisdiction extends to "customs waters." These waters include the three-mile territorial limit of the United States (P) as well as the ships of any nation which has agreed by treaty to permit U.S. inspection. Here, Panama had entered into such a treaty with the United States (P), so the fact that the "El Don" was on the high seas at the time of inspection was of no moment; it was in U.S. customs waters. Therefore, § 955a(c) is applicable. Reversed.

ANALYSIS

The rule invoked here probably did not need a treaty to be effective. Under the "protective principle," a nation may extend its jurisdiction beyond its borders. The smuggling of narcotics would, in most circumstances, be seen as a sufficient threat to state security so as to invoke the protective principle.

Quicknotes

TREATY An agreement between two or more nations for the benefit of the general public.

United States v. Columba-Colella

Federal government (P) v. British citizen (D)

604 F.2d 356 (5th Cir. 1979).

NATURE OF CASE: Appeal of conviction of receiving a stolen vehicle in foreign commerce.

FACT SUMMARY: Columba-Colella (D), a British citizen, was convicted of receiving a stolen vehicle in foreign commerce, even though he had no part in the actual stealing of the vehicle in the United States (P).

RULE OF LAW

A foreigner cannot be convicted of receiving a stolen vehicle in foreign commerce if he had no part in the actual stealing of the vehicle in the United States.

FACTS: Columba-Colella (D) was a British citizen residing in Mexico. At one point he became acquainted with Keith, a U.S. citizen. Keith told him that he possessed a vehicle that had been stolen in the United States (P), and asked him if he would find a buyer. Columba-Colella (D) agreed and took possession of the vehicle. He was later arrested by Mexican police and turned over to U.S. authorities. He was convicted under 18 U.S.C. § 2313, which proscribes receiving a stolen vehicle in foreign commerce. Columba-Colella (D) appealed.

ISSUE: Can a foreigner be convicted of receiving a stolen vehicle in foreign commerce if he had no part in the actual stealing of the vehicle in the United States?

HOLDING AND DECISION: (Wisdom, J.) No. A foreigner cannot be convicted of receiving a stolen vehicle in foreign commerce if he had no part in the actual stealing of the vehicle in the United States. When an allegedly criminal act occurs on foreign soil and is committed by someone not a U.S. national, jurisdiction can be supported only by the protective or the objective territorial theories. The former, dealing with national security, is not germane here. The second basis for jurisdiction looks to objective effects within the sovereign state. An act done outside the jurisdiction with the intent and result of producing an effect in the state will provide a basis for extraterritorial reach. Here, Columba-Colella's (D) acts occurred after the vehicle had been stolen from the United States; the effects felt in the United States (P) had already occurred. As a consequence, the objective territorial principle does not apply, and jurisdiction did not extend to his actions. Reversed.

ANALYSIS

In 1984, perhaps in partial response to the present case, § 2313 was amended. The statute now penalizes possession of a vehicle "which has crossed a . . . United States boundary after being stolen." This would seem to show a congressional intent to have application in a situation such as that presented here, but as to whether such extraterritorial application would violate international law is a question which has not yet been answered.

Quicknotes

JURISDICTION The authority of a court to hear and declare judgment in respect to a particular matter.

SOVEREIGN A state or entity with independent authority to govern its affairs.

Pancotto v. Sociedade de Safaris de Mozambique, S.A.R.L.

Injured (P) v. Foreign corporation (D)

422 F. Supp. 405 (N.D. Ill. 1976).

NATURE OF CASE: Action for damages for personal injuries.

FACT SUMMARY: Pancotto (P), suing a foreign corporation for personal injuries sustained outside the United States, contended that the law of the forum state should apply because a failure to do so would result in inadequate compensation.

RULE OF LAW

The law of a forum state may be applied to an extraterritorial accident if applying local law would result in inadequate compensation.

FACTS: Pancotto (P) was injured in an accident while on a tour organized by Sociedade de Safaris de Mozambique (D). She brought suit in federal district court in Illinois, jurisdiction predicated on diversity. The issue arose as to whether the law of the injury situs, Mozambique, or of the forum, Illinois, should apply. The court first concluded that the forum state's choice of law rules would apply. Illinois followed the Restatement rule, which identified four factors: place of injury, place of conduct causing injury, domicile of the parties, and place of the parties' relationship. The court concluded that Mozambique law should apply. The court then addressed Pancotto's (P) contention that since Mozambique law contained a limitation on liability which would result in insignificant compensation, Illinois law should be followed as to damages.

ISSUE: May the law of a forum state be applied to an extraterritorial accident if applying local law would result in inadequate compensation?

HOLDING AND DECISION: (Marshall, J.) Yes. The law of a forum state may be applied to an extraterritorial accident if applying local law would result in inadequate compensation. The factors to be analyzed as to damages are the same as those to be analyzed as to liability. No Illinois case exists as to whether the factors may be analyzed differently with respect to the former and the latter. However, Illinois has a strong interest in seeing to it that its citizens are adequately compensated a lawsuit; in fact, this right is codified in the state constitution. Absent an articulated national policy to the contrary in the defendant country, evidence of which has not been presented here, this court believes that Illinois courts would refuse to enforce the damage limitation found in Mozambique law. Reversed.

ANALYSIS

The source of conflicts law in this case was the Illinois decision *Ingersoll v. Klein*, 46 Ill. 2d 42 (1970). *Ingersoll* applied the majority rule with respect to choice-of-law issues. This rule may be found in § 145 of the Restatement (Second) of Conflicts. In this federal case, Illinois law was being followed because it was a diversity action.

Quicknotes

DAMAGES Monetary compensation that may be awarded by the court to a party who has sustained injury or loss to his or her person, property or rights due to another party's unlawful act, omission or negligence.

DIVERSITY ACTION An action commenced by a citizen of one state against a citizen of another state or against an alien, involving an amount in controversy of $10,000 or more, over which the federal court has jurisdiction.

CHAPTER 8

International Human Rights and Responsibility for Injuries to Aliens

Quick Reference Rules of Law

Case of Schalk and Kopf v. Austria

Same-sex Couple (P) v. Member State of European Union (D)

European Court of Human Rights, 49 ILM 1306 (2010).

NATURE OF CASE: Consideration of plaintiffs' complaint alleging violations of the Articles of the European Convention on Human Rights.

FACT SUMMARY: Schalk (P) and Kopf (P), a same-sex couple from Vienna, Austria, sought a marriage license in Austria. Municipal officials denied their request. Austria (D) later enacted a Registered Partnership Act providing same-sex couples with some of the benefits of marriage.

RULE OF LAW

The Articles of the European Convention do not currently require that member states allow same-sex couples access to marriage.

FACTS: In 2002, Schalk (P) and Kopf (P), a same-sex couple, applied for a marriage license in Vienna, Austria. City officials denied their request. In 2010, Austria promulgated the Registered Partnership Act. The Act gives same-sex couples a mechanism to give their relationship legal status. While the Act gives same-sex couples some of the benefits of marriage, it does not allow same-sex couples to adopt children. The complaint alleges that the denial of a marriage license violates Articles 8, 12, and 14 of the Convention.

ISSUE: Do the Articles of the European Convention currently require that member states allow same-sex couples access to marriage?

HOLDING AND DECISION: [Judge not stated in casebook excerpt.] No. The Articles of the European Convention (the Convention) do not currently require that member states allow same-sex couples access to marriage. First, the plaintiffs contend the denial of the marriage license violates Article 12. Article 12 states, "Men and women of marriageable age have the right to marry and to found a family, according to the national laws governing the exercise of this right." Schalk (P) and Kopf (P) argue the language does not per se bar same-sex couples from marrying. However, elsewhere the Articles use the terms "everyone" and "no one," rather than men and women. Use of the term "men and women" must be regarded as deliberate to define marriage as only a relationship between a man and a woman. Also, there is no present day consensus regarding same-sex marriage. Only six of the 47 member states allow same-sex marriage. This Court is of the opinion that the issue of same-sex marriage is one best left to the member states to decide. Schalk (P) and Kopf (P) also claim the denial of a marriage license violates Articles 14 and 8 of the Convention. Article 8 states that "everyone has the right to respect for his private and family life." Article 14 then states that the enjoyment of these rights shall not be discriminated against "on any ground such as sex, race, color and language," among other criteria. Schalk (P) and Kopf (P) argue that Austria (D) provided no reason for their denial. In addition, they claim Austria (D) provided no legal justification for unequal treatment of same-sex couples via the Registered Partnership Act. The member states enjoy a margin of appreciation when deciding to treat their own residents differently. The scope of that margin will depend on the subject matter of the classification. Here, having found that Article 12 does not impose an obligation on member states to recognize same-sex marriage, there can be no valid discrimination claim pursuant to Article 14 and 8. Accordingly, the court holds unanimously that Article 12 has not been violated. The Court holds four votes to three that Article 14 and 8 have not been violated.

DISSENT: (Rozarkis, J., Speilmann, J., Jebens, J.) The Court should have found a violation of Article 14 and 8 because Austria (D) failed to provide any legitimate basis for the difference in treatment of same-sex couples via the Registered Partnership Act. Austria (D) relies solely on the "margin of appreciation" afforded member states when classifying their own residents. However, that margin of appreciation should not protect a state when it fails to provide any reasons whatsoever for the difference in treatment.

ANALYSIS

While there is a debate in the United States whether the U.S. Constitution is a "living document," the European Court has recognized that the Articles of the Convention should be viewed as a living document and, accordingly, interpreted in light of present day social norms. Accordingly, as more member states allow same-sex marriages, future consideration of this issue by the European Court may yield a different result. Separately, the United States Supreme Court may take up same-sex marriages in its 2011–2012 term.

Quicknotes

DISCRIMINATION Unequal treatment of a class of persons.

CHAPTER 9

Law of the Sea

Quick Reference Rules of Law

Lauritzen v. Larsen

Shipowner (D) v. Sailor (P)

345 U.S. 571 (1953).

NATURE OF CASE: Appeal of award of damages for personal injury.

FACT SUMMARY: Lauritzen (D) contended that, in a sailor's action for personal injury under the Jones Act, the law of the nation of registry, Denmark, should apply.

RULE OF LAW

In an action under the Jones Act, the law of the nation of registry will be presumed to apply.

FACTS: Larsen (P), a Danish seaman, was injured on a merchant ship, "Randa," which was registered with Denmark. He brought an action against Lauritzen (D) [whose connection with the accident was not explained in the casebook excerpt] under the Jones Act, a federal law affording seamen a right of action for personal injuries. Lauritzen (D) contended that Danish, not U.S., law should apply. The district court ruled U.S. law to control. The damages awarded were affirmed by the Second Circuit Court of Appeals, and the United States Supreme Court accepted review.

ISSUE: In an action under the Jones Act, will the law of the nation of registry be presumed to apply?

HOLDING AND DECISION: (Jackson, J.) Yes. In an action under the Jones Act, the law of the nation of registry will be presumed to apply. The law of the flag supersedes the territorial principle because it is deemed to be part of the territory of the registering nation and not to lose that character when in the territorial limits of another nation. This principle is recognized in international law and is settled in American doctrine. Consequently, the registering nation will be presumed to have the highest interest in an action for injuries occurring on the ship, and a heavy countervailing interest will have to be shown to upset this presumption. None has been shown here. Reversed.

ANALYSIS

At least two conceptual bases exist for the rule announced here. The first is that the ship is, in effect, a floating piece of the flag state. The other is the more pragmatic notion that a crew cannot be expected to subscribe to potentially different laws every time it arrives at a different port. The Court here seemed to prefer the prior concept, although the result is the same under either approach.

Quicknotes

JONES ACT Extended mineral rights to previously granted lands.

PRESUMPTION A rule of law requiring the court to presume certain facts to be true based on the existence of other facts, thereby shifting the burden of proof to the party against whom the presumption is asserted to rebut.

Fisheries Case (United Kingdom v. Norway)

United Kingdom (P) v. Norway (D)

Intl. Ct. of Justice, 1951 I.C.J. 116 (Dec. 18, 1951).

NATURE OF CASE: Dispute between states with respect to demarcation of territorial waters.

FACT SUMMARY: Norway (D), in determining its territorial waters, employed a baselines method of computation rather than a parallel-tracing method.

RULE OF LAW

A nation may use a baselines method of computing the boundaries of its territorial waters, if parallelism cannot be practically employed.

FACTS: Since 1618, England (P) had refrained from fishing in Norwegian coastal waters. In 1909, however, British vessels began trawling off the coast of Norway in search of fish catches. The Norwegian government (D) complained from time to time, and occasionally British merchant ships were seized and condemned. In 1935, the Norwegian government (D) entered a decree which purported to establish the territorial limits of Norwegian coastal limits. Norway's (D) coast was extremely jagged, containing literally thousands of fjords, islands, archipelagos, inlets, and peninsulas. Rather than tracing the territorial demarcation parallel to each geographical feature, Norway (D) drew certain baselines connecting significant geographical features along the coast. Britain (P) eventually brought an action in the International Court of Justice, contending that the method used by Norway (D) violated international law.

ISSUE: May a nation use a baselines method of computing the boundaries of its territorial waters, if parallelism cannot be practically employed?

HOLDING AND DECISION: [Judge not stated in casebook excerpt.] Yes. A nation may use a baselines method of computing the boundaries of its territorial waters, if parallelism cannot be practically employed. The normal procedure for a nation to demarcate the limits of its territorial waters is by parallel tracing along the coast of that country. However, in a situation involving a jagged coastline, practical difficulties arise in the computation of what is parallel that make such a method impossible to follow. In such circumstances, states have traditionally drawn a series of straight lines roughly following the direction of the coast, and no serious protest of this practice has arisen in the international community. In assessing the validity of the laying of such boundaries, certain factors must be borne in mind. One is the dependence of the sea upon the land domain, which is to say, the drawing of baselines must roughly follow the direction of the coast. Another consideration is the extent to which the land and sea are interrelated, which is to say, the more jagged the coast the less absolute parallelism will be required. Finally, the historical claim of the nation at issue on the coastal waters is relevant. Here, all these considerations weigh in favor of Norway's (D) 1935 decree: the general direction of the coast is followed, the coast is extremely jagged, and Norway (D) has historically exercised dominion over the coast in conformity with the areas covered by the decree. Consequently, the decree would appear to be in conformity with international law. Judgment for Norway (D).

ANALYSIS

The accepted rule in international law is that the territorial boundary of a nation extends a set distance from the mean low water mark of the coast. The distance such territory extends has varied in different situations. The usual figure is three miles, although for reasons not explained in the opinion the parties here agreed to a four-mile breadth.

Quicknotes

TERRITORIAL WATERS That portion of the sea that is within three miles of a nation's coast and over which that nation has jurisdiction.

North Sea Continental Shelf Cases (Federal Republic of Germany v. Denmark; Federal Republic of Germany v. Netherlands)

[Parties not identified.]

Int'l Ct. of Justice, I.C.J. Rep. 1 (Feb. 20, 1969).

NATURE OF CASE: Delimitation of boundaries.

FACT SUMMARY: The Federal Republic of Germany and the Netherlands and Denmark had a dispute regarding the delimitation of the boundaries of their respective continental shelves in the North Sea.

RULE OF LAW

Delimitation is to be effected by agreement in accordance with equitable principles, and taking account of all the relevant circumstances, in such a way as to leave as much possible to each party all those parts of the continental shelf that constitute a natural prolongation of its land territory into and under the sea, without encroachment on the natural prolongation of the land territory of the other.

FACTS: The Federal Republic of Germany and the Netherlands and Denmark had a dispute regarding the delimitation of the boundaries of their respective continental shelves in the North Sea. The countries applied to the International Court of Justice to resolve the issue. The court rejected the argument of Denmark and the Netherlands that the rule of equidistance applied.

ISSUE: Is delimitation to be effected by agreement in accordance with equitable principles, and taking account of all the relevant circumstances, in such a way as to leave as much possible to each party all those parts of the continental shelf that constitute a natural prolongation of its land territory into and under the sea, without encroachment on the natural prolongation of the land territory of the other?

HOLDING AND DECISION: [Judge not stated in casebook excerpt.] Yes. Delimitation is to be effected by agreement in accordance with equitable principles, and taking account of all the relevant circumstances, in such a way as to leave as much possible to each party all those parts of the continental shelf that constitute a natural prolongation of its land territory into and under the sea, without encroachment on the natural prolongation of the land territory of the other. If the delimitation leaves to the parties areas that overlap, these are to be divided between them in agreed proportions or, failing agreement, equally, unless they decide on joint jurisdiction, user, or exploitation for the overlapping zones.

ANALYSIS

Factors to be considered in the negotiations were to include: (1) the configuration of the coast of the countries, including any unusual features; (2) the physiological and geological structure and natural resources of the regions involved; and (3) a reasonable degree of proportionality.

Quicknotes

EQUITABLE Just; fair.

CHAPTER 10

International Environmental Law

Quick Reference Rules of Law

Trail Smelter Case (United States v. Canada)

United States (P) v. Canada (D)

Arbitral Trib., 1941, III U.N. Rep. Intl. Arb. Awards 1905, 1962–1966 (1950).

NATURE OF CASE: Action for damages for air pollution.

FACT SUMMARY: The United States (P) brought this action against Canada (D) seeking damages and an injunction for air pollution, in the state of Washington, by the Trail Smelter, a Canadian corporation located in Canada.

RULE OF LAW

A state owes, at all times, a duty to protect other states against injurious acts by individuals from within its jurisdiction.

FACTS: Since 1906, the Trail Smelter, located in British Columbia, was owned and operated by a Canadian corporation. From 1925, at least, to 1937, damage occurred in the state of Washington, resulting from the sulfur dioxide from the Trail Smelter. The United States (P) brought an action for damages against Canada and also sought an injunction against further air pollution by the Trail Smelter.

ISSUE: Does a state owe a duty to protect other states against injurious acts by individuals from within its jurisdiction?

HOLDING AND DECISION: [Judge not stated in casebook excerpt.] Yes. A state owes, at all times, a duty to protect other states against injurious acts by individuals from within its jurisdiction. Under the principles of international law, as well as the law of the United States (P), no state has the right to use or permit the use of the territory in a manner as to cause injury by fumes in or to the territory of another or the properties or persons therein. Considering the facts of the case, this tribunal holds that Canada (D) is responsible in international law for the conduct of the Trail Smelter. It is, therefore, the duty of the government of Canada (D) to see to it that the Trail Smelter's conduct should be in conformity with the obligations of Canada (D) under international law as herein determined. So long as the present conditions of air pollution exist in Washington, the Trail Smelter shall be required to refrain from causing any damage through fumes. The indemnity for damage should be fixed by the governments of the United States (P) and Canada (D) pursuant to Article III of the convention existing between the two nations. Lastly, since this tribunal is of the opinion that damage may occur in the future unless the operations of the smelter shall be subject to some control, a regime or measure of control shall be applied to the operations of the smelter.

ANALYSIS

It is interesting to note that no international tribunal has ever held a state responsible for pollution of the sea or held that there exists a duty to desist from polluting the seas. The international regulation of pollution is just beginning, and the regulation must always be balanced against freedom of the seas guaranteed under general and long-established rules of international law.

Quicknotes

DAMAGES Monetary compensation that may be awarded by the court to a party who has sustained injury or loss to his or her person, property, or rights due to another party's unlawful act, omission, or negligence.

DUTY An obligation owed by one individual to another.

INJUNCTION A court order requiring a person to do or prohibiting that person from doing a specific act.

Natural Resources Defense Council v. Environmental Protection Agency

Environmental protection group (P) v. Government agency (D)

464 F.3d 1 (D.C. Cir. 2006).

NATURE OF CASE: Challenge of international council's decision as "law."

FACT SUMMARY: [Facts not stated in casebook excerpt.]

RULE OF LAW

Without congressional action, side agreements reached after a treaty has been ratified are not law that is enforceable through the courts.

FACTS: [Facts not stated in casebook excerpt.]

ISSUE: Without congressional action, are side agreements reached after a treaty has been ratified law that is enforceable through the courts?

HOLDING AND DECISION: [Judge not stated in casebook excerpt.] No. Without congressional action, side agreements reached after a treaty has been ratified are not law that is enforceable through the courts. Enforcing the decisions as law would mean that Congress has either delegated lawmaking authority to an international body, or authorized amendments to a treaty without presidential signature or Senate ratification, in violation of the Constitution. The provisions of the Montreal Protocol setting limits on methyl bromide constitute an "agreement to agree," which is not enforceable under contract law.

ANALYSIS

In this case, the Natural Resources Defense Council (P) challenged the Environmental Protection Agency's (EPA's) (D) rule addressing methyl bromide, a substance that was also controlled by the Montreal Protocol. The National Resources Defense Council (P) argued that the Environmental Protection Agency (D) violated a "decision" of the Council of the Parties to the Montreal Convention.

Note: There are no principal cases in Chapter 11 of the casebook.

CHAPTER 12

International Criminal Law

Quick Reference Rules of Law

Arrest Warrant of 11 April 2000 (Democratic Republic of the Congo v. Belgium)

State (P) v. Incumbent foreign minister (D)

Int'l. Ct. of Justice, 2002 I.C.J. 3, (Feb. 14, 2002).

NATURE OF CASE: Jurisdictional question.

FACT SUMMARY: [Facts not stated in casebook excerpt.]

RULE OF LAW

Incumbent Ministers for Foreign Affairs are immune from criminal suit abroad, notwithstanding allegations of having committed war crimes or crimes against humanity.

FACTS: [Facts not stated in casebook excerpt.]

ISSUE: Are incumbent Ministers of Foreign Affairs immune from criminal suit abroad, notwithstanding having committed war crimes or crimes against humanity?

HOLDING AND DECISION: [Judge not stated in casebook excerpt.] Yes. Incumbent Ministers for Foreign Affairs are immune from criminal suit abroad, notwithstanding allegations of having committed war crimes or crimes against humanity. Written international law provides no exception to the rule granting immunity from criminal jurisdiction to incumbent Ministers for Foreign Affairs, where they are suspected of having committed war crimes or crimes against humanity, but immunity from jurisdiction is not equivalent to impunity for crimes that have been committed. Immunity from criminal jurisdiction and individual criminal responsibility are distinct concepts. While jurisdictional immunity is procedural in nature, criminal responsibility is a question of substantive law. Jurisdictional immunity may well bar prosecution for a certain period or for certain offences; it cannot exonerate the person to whom it applies from all criminal responsibility. First, heads of state enjoy no criminal immunity under international law in their own countries, and thus may be tried by those countries' courts in accordance with the relevant rules of domestic law. Second, they will cease to enjoy immunity from foreign jurisdiction if the state they represent or have represented decides to waive that immunity. Third, after a person ceases to hold the office of Minister for Foreign Affairs, he or she will no longer enjoy all of the immunities accorded by international law in other states. Fourth, an incumbent or former Minister for Foreign Affairs may be subject to criminal proceedings before certain international criminal courts, where they have jurisdiction.

ANALYSIS

In *Regina v. Bow Street Metropolitan Stipendiary Magistrate and Others, Ex Parte Pinochet Ugarte*, [2000] 1 A.C. 147, 201-202 (H.L. 1999), the British House of Lords abrogated Augusto Pinochet's immunity under international law as a former head of state, declaring him subject to extradition for the crime of torture. The main holding of *Congo v. Belgium* is technically consistent with *Pinochet*, insofar as the ICJ ruled on the immunity of incumbent rather than former officials. The reasoning of the ICJ, however, is in serious tension with that of the Law Lords, and the opinion could even be read as a rejection of *Pinochet*. *Pinochet* was considered by many to represent a major shift in international law respecting official immunity, but the ICJ opinion in *Democratic Republic of Congo v. Belgium* casts doubt on this belief.

Quicknotes

IMMUNITY Exemption from a legal obligation.

In re Yamashita

Japanese general (D) v. American military (P)

327 U.S. 1 (1946).

NATURE OF CASE: Appeal by Japanese general of conviction for war crime.

FACT SUMMARY: Yamashita (D) failed to stop his command from committing crimes against people of the United States and the Philippines. He did not commit the crimes himself.

RULE OF LAW

The law of war imposes on an army commander a duty to prevent his troops from committing acts that violate the law of war.

FACTS: Yamashita (D) failed to stop his command from committing crimes against people of the United States (P) and the Philippines in the wake of World War II. He may not have committed the crimes, ordered them, condoned them, or even known about them. He was charged by an American military commission (P) only with neglecting an affirmative duty to take measures to protect prisoners of war and the civilian population from his troops.

ISSUE: Does the law of war impose on an army commander a duty to prevent his troops from committing acts that violate the law of war?

HOLDING AND DECISION: (Stone, C.J.) Yes. The law of war imposes on an army commander a duty to prevent his troops from committing acts that violate the law of war. The law of war's purpose is to protect civilian populations and prisoners of war from brutality that occurs most often in occupied territories, and that purpose would be defeated if the commander could with impunity neglect to take reasonable measures for their protection. The Annex to the Fourth Hague Convention of 1907 recognizes this rule.

DISSENT: (Murphy, J.) Yamashita (D) was not charged with personally participating in the acts or with ordering or condoning their commission, or even with knowing that they occurred. The charges are without precedent. The military commissions made up the crime, according to its own biases.

ANALYSIS

Yamashita commanded around 262,000 troops. Just before the Battle of Manila, he was forced to retreat to the mountains of northern Luzon, and left with all but a security force of around 3,750 troops. Almost immediately, Rear Admiral Sanji Iwabuchi of the Imperial Japanese Navy reoccupied Manila with 16,000 sailors. Once there, Iwabuchi took command of the 3,750 Army security troops, and against Yamashita's specific order, turned on the city. In what would later be called the "Manila Massacre," the Japanese garrison killed more than 100,000 Filipino civilians from February 4 to March 3. The American military commission tried General Yamashita for war crimes related to the Manila Massacre from October 29 to December 7, 1945. He was sentenced to death. This case has become a precedent regarding the command responsibility for war crimes and is known as the Yamashita Standard. Nevertheless, the legitimacy of the trial has been called into question by many, because Yamashita was either not aware of the actions of the garrison, or was unable to control his soldiers properly due to communication disruption caused by the U.S. Army during their offensive. One of the atrocities in Manila was committed by a unit that disobeyed his orders to retreat, and most of the others belonged to the Imperial Japanese Navy, which was not under his command.

Quicknotes

WAR Hostilities between nations.

Prosecutor v. Furundžija

State (P) v. Accused war criminal (D)

Int'l. Crim. Tribunal for the former Yugoslavia, Case No. IT-95-17/1-T, Judgment (Dec. 10, 1998).

NATURE OF CASE: Trial of soldier accused of aiding and abetting a war crime.

FACT SUMMARY: [Facts not stated in casebook excerpt.]

RULE OF LAW

The elements of aiding and abetting in international criminal law are providing practical assistance, encouragement, or moral support which has a substantial effect on the perpetration of the crime, with knowledge that these acts assist the commission of the offense.

FACTS: [Facts not stated in casebook excerpt.]

ISSUE: Are the elements of aiding and abetting in international criminal law providing practical assistance, encouragement, or moral support which has a substantial effect on the perpetration of the crime, with knowledge that these acts assist the commission of the offense?

HOLDING AND DECISION: [Judge not identified in casebook excerpt.] Yes. The elements of aiding and abetting in international criminal law are providing practical assistance, encouragement, or moral support which has a substantial effect on the perpetration of the crime, with knowledge that these acts assist the commission of the offense. He need not share with the principal perpetrator the intention to commit the crime, but to have knowledge that his actions will assist the perpetrator in the commission of the crime.

ANALYSIS

The appeals chamber did not consider the issue of whether mere presence, or knowing presence, constitutes aiding and abetting, because the Furundžija (D) had interrogated the witness during the commission of the crime. Whether "interrogation" has a substantial effect on commission of the crime also was not addressed by the chamber, but without explanation.

Quicknotes

AIDING AND ABETTING Assistance given in order to facilitate the commission of a criminal act.

WAR CRIMES Crimes committed by nations during war in violation of international law.

Prosecutor v. Krstić

International criminal tribunal (P) v. Alleged war criminal (D)

Int'l. Crim. Tribunal for the former Yugoslavia, IT-98-33-A, Judgment of the Appeals Chamber (April 19, 2004).

NATURE OF CASE: Appeal of conviction for war crime.

FACT SUMMARY: Radislav Krstić was charged with genocide for the killing of approximately 10,000 Bosnian men and boys in the Muslim community of Srebrenica, which is in eastern Bosnia. Krstić knew of the intention on the part of the VRS military commander and other members of the army to execute the Bosnian Muslims of Srebrenica, and of the use of Drina Corps (which he commanded) to carry out that intention, and that he supervised the participation of his subordinates in carrying out the executions. His contacts with the officers who were the main participants in the executions established only that Krstić was aware that the executions were taking place.

RULE OF LAW

A commander's knowledge that mass executions are taking place with the help of his command is insufficient to support an inference that he shared the intent to commit genocide.

FACTS: Radislav Krstić was charged with genocide for the killing of approximately 10,000 Bosnian men and boys in the Muslim community of Srebrenica, which is in eastern Bosnia. The Trial Chamber found that Krstić possessed genocidal intent through evidence establishing his knowledge of the intention on the part of the VRS military commander and other members of the army to execute the Bosnian Muslims of Srebrenica, his knowledge of the use of personnel and resources of the Drina Corps (which he commanded) to carry out that intention, and that Krstić supervised the participation of his subordinates in carrying out the executions. His contacts with the officers who were the main participants in the executions established only that Krstić was aware that the executions were taking place.

ISSUE: Is a commander's knowledge that mass executions are taking place with the help of his command sufficient to support an inference that he shared the intent to commit genocide?

HOLDING AND DECISION: [Judge not stated in casebook excerpt.] No. A commander's knowledge that mass executions are taking place with the help of his command is insufficient to support an inference that he shared the intent to commit genocide. The killing of the Bosnian Muslim men and boys was done with genocidal intent. But that intent cannot be attributed to Krstić, because the evidence only established that he was aware of the intent to commit genocide, and he did nothing to prevent the use of his command to facilitate those killings. Knowledge alone cannot support an inference of intent. By allowing the use of Drina Corps, he knew he was making a substantial contribution to the execution of the prisoners, but he is at most an aider and abettor to genocide, and not a perpetrator of genocide.

ANALYSIS

On August 2, 2001, Krstić became the first man convicted of genocide by the International Criminal Tribunal, and was sentenced to 46 years in prison, which was reduced by the Appeals Chamber in 2004, when he was found guilty of the lesser crime of aiding and abetting genocide. He was only the third person ever to have been convicted under the 1948 Convention on the Prevention and Punishment of the Crime of Genocide.

Quicknotes

AIDING AND ABETTING Assistance given in order to facilitate the commission of a criminal act.

GENOCIDE The systematic killing of a particular group.

WAR CRIMES Crimes committed by nations during war in violation of international law.

Prosecutor v. Kunarac et al., Case No. IT-96-23 & 23/1

International prosecutor (P) v. Members of the Bosnian Serb military (D)

Int't. Crim. Tribunal for the Former Yugoslavia, Appeals Judgment (June 12, 2002).

NATURE OF CASE: Appeal from trial court's conviction of the defendants for crimes against humanity.

FACT SUMMARY: Kunarac (D) and other defendants were members of the Bosnian Serb military that in 1992 killed, raped, and tortured non-Serb civilians.

RULE OF LAW

To state a claim for a crime against humanity, the defendant's acts must be part of a widespread or systematic attack directed against a civilian population, and the defendant must know that his acts are part of the attack.

FACTS: In 1992 and 1993, Kunarac (D) and other members of the Bosian Serb military engaged in a series of acts, including rape, torture, and murder, against non-Serb civilians. In particular, Kunarac (D) and others brought Muslim women to "centers" where they were raped multiple times and subjected to other acts of physical violence. The trial chamber of the International Criminal Tribune found Kunarac (D) guilty of multiple counts of enslavement, rape and torture. Kunarac (D) appealed on the grounds there was no "attack" against non-Serb civilians, that the non-Serb civilians were not a "population," the attack was not widespread or systematic, and that he had no knowledge of an attack or the policy behind it.

ISSUE: To state a claim for a crime against humanity, must the defendant's acts be part of a widespread or systematic attack directed against a civilian population, and must the defendant know that his acts are part of the attack?

HOLDING AND DECISION: [Judge not stated in casebook excerpt.) Yes. To state a claim for a crime against humanity, the defendant's acts must be part of a widespread or systematic attack directed against a civilian population, and the defendant must know that his acts are part of the attack. First, the term "attack" is interpreted broadly. It is not limited to use of armed military forces—it includes any mistreatment of civilians. Regarding the term "population," the statute only requires a showing that the attack was not limited to a select and randomly chosen group of individuals. The term "directed against" a civilian population means that an attack against civilians is the primary object of the attack. A court should review the means and methods of the attack, the status of the victims, and the nature of the crimes. The attack must be widespread *or* systematic. Widespread means on a large scale. Systematic means an organized pattern to the violence. Only the general attack, and not the specific acts of the individual charged, need be widespread or systematic. Also, the prosecutor need not prove that there was a "policy" or plan behind the attacks. The individual acts of the accused must be part of the attack however. Isolated acts not related to an attack may not qualify. Lastly, the prosecutor must prove the defendant had the intent to commit his own specific criminal acts. The defendant must also know his acts were part of the attack directed against the civilian population. It is irrelevant whether the defendant intended his acts to be directed against the population or his victim. It is the general attack that must be directed against the population. Affirmed.

ANALYSIS

There has been much debate over the nature of the mens rea element required for crimes against humanity. Obviously, a prosecutor must prove that a defendant had the intent to the commit the underlying acts of which he is accused. However, the mens rea required for the general crimes against humanity charge is much lower. The defendant need only have knowledge that his acts are part of a general attack against a civilian population, even if he does not share the motivation or does not intend his own acts to be an attack against the population generally.

Quicknotes

MENS REA Criminal intent.

Glossary

Common Latin Words and Phrases Encountered in the Law

A FORTIORI: Because one fact exists or has been proven, therefore a second fact that is related to the first fact must also exist.

A PRIORI: From the cause to the effect. A term of logic used to denote that when one generally accepted truth is shown to be a cause, another particular effect must necessarily follow.

AB INITIO: From the beginning; a condition which has existed throughout, as in a marriage which was void ab initio.

ACTUS REUS: The wrongful act; in criminal law, such action sufficient to trigger criminal liability.

AD VALOREM: According to value; an ad valorem tax is imposed upon an item located within the taxing jurisdiction calculated by the value of such item.

AMICUS CURIAE: Friend of the court. Its most common usage takes the form of an amicus curiae brief, filed by a person who is not a party to an action but is nonetheless allowed to offer an argument supporting his legal interests.

ARGUENDO: In arguing. A statement, possibly hypothetical, made for the purpose of argument, is one made arguendo.

BILL QUIA TIMET: A bill to quiet title (establish ownership) to real property.

BONA FIDE: True, honest, or genuine. May refer to a person's legal position based on good faith or lacking notice of fraud (such as a bona fide purchaser for value) or to the authenticity of a particular document (such as a bona fide last will and testament).

CAUSA MORTIS: With approaching death in mind. A gift causa mortis is a gift given by a party who feels certain that death is imminent.

CAVEAT EMPTOR: Let the buyer beware. This maxim is reflected in the rule of law that a buyer purchases at his own risk because it is his responsibility to examine, judge, test, and otherwise inspect what he is buying.

CERTIORARI: A writ of review. Petitions for review of a case by the United States Supreme Court are most often done by means of a writ of certiorari.

CONTRA: On the other hand. Opposite. Contrary to.

CORAM NOBIS: Before us; writs of error directed to the court that originally rendered the judgment.

CORAM VOBIS: Before you; writs of error directed by an appellate court to a lower court to correct a factual error.

CORPUS DELICTI: The body of the crime; the requisite elements of a crime amounting to objective proof that a crime has been committed.

CUM TESTAMENTO ANNEXO, ADMINISTRATOR (ADMINISTRATOR C.T.A.): With will annexed; an administrator c.t.a. settles an estate pursuant to a will in which he is not appointed.

DE BONIS NON, ADMINISTRATOR (ADMINISTRATOR D.B.N.): Of goods not administered; an administrator d.b.n. settles a partially settled estate.

DE FACTO: In fact; in reality; actually. Existing in fact but not officially approved or engendered.

DE JURE: By right; lawful. Describes a condition that is legitimate "as a matter of law," in contrast to the term "de facto," which connotes something existing in fact but not legally sanctioned or authorized. For example, de facto segregation refers to segregation brought about by housing patterns, etc., whereas de jure segregation refers to segregation created by law.

DE MINIMIS: Of minimal importance; insignificant; a trifle; not worth bothering about.

DE NOVO: Anew; a second time; afresh. A trial de novo is a new trial held at the appellate level as if the case originated there and the trial at a lower level had not taken place.

DICTA: Generally used as an abbreviated form of obiter dicta, a term describing those portions of a judicial opinion incidental or not necessary to resolution of the specific question before the court. Such nonessential statements and remarks are not considered to be binding precedent.

DUCES TECUM: Refers to a particular type of writ or subpoena requesting a party or organization to produce certain documents in their possession.

EN BANC: Full bench. Where a court sits with all justices present rather than the usual quorum.

EX PARTE: For one side or one party only. An ex parte proceeding is one undertaken for the benefit of only one party, without notice to, or an appearance by, an adverse party.

EX POST FACTO: After the fact. An ex post facto law is a law that retroactively changes the consequences of a prior act.

EX REL.: Abbreviated form of the term "ex relatione," meaning upon relation or information. When the state brings an action in which it has no interest against an individual at the instigation of one who has a private interest in the matter.

FORUM NON CONVENIENS: Inconvenient forum. Although a court may have jurisdiction over the case, the action should be tried in a more conveniently located court, one to which parties and witnesses may more easily travel, for example.

GUARDIAN AD LITEM: A guardian of an infant as to litigation, appointed to represent the infant and pursue his/her rights.

HABEAS CORPUS: You have the body. The modern writ of habeas corpus is a writ directing that a person (body) being detained (such as a prisoner) be brought before the court so that the legality of his detention can be judicially ascertained.

IN CAMERA: In private, in chambers. When a hearing is held before a judge in his chambers or when all spectators are excluded from the courtroom.

IN FORMA PAUPERIS: In the manner of a pauper. A party who proceeds in forma pauperis because of his poverty is one who is allowed to bring suit without liability for costs.

INFRA: Below, under. A word referring the reader to a later part of a book. (The opposite of supra.)

IN LOCO PARENTIS: In the place of a parent.

IN PARI DELICTO: Equally wrong; a court of equity will not grant requested relief to an applicant who is in pari delicto, or as much at fault in the transactions giving rise to the controversy as is the opponent of the applicant.

IN PARI MATERIA: On like subject matter or upon the same matter. Statutes relating to the same person or things are said to be in pari materia. It is a general rule of statutory construction that such statutes should be construed together, i.e., looked at as if they together constituted one law.

IN PERSONAM: Against the person. Jurisdiction over the person of an individual.

IN RE: In the matter of. Used to designate a proceeding involving an estate or other property.

IN REM: A term that signifies an action against the res, or thing. An action in rem is basically one that is taken directly against property, as distinguished from an action in personam, i.e., against the person.

INTER ALIA: Among other things. Used to show that the whole of a statement, pleading, list, statute, etc., has not been set forth in its entirety.

INTER PARTES: Between the parties. May refer to contracts, conveyances or other transactions having legal significance.

INTER VIVOS: Between the living. An inter vivos gift is a gift made by a living grantor, as distinguished from bequests contained in a will, which pass upon the death of the testator.

IPSO FACTO: By the mere fact itself.

JUS: Law or the entire body of law.

LEX LOCI: The law of the place; the notion that the rights of parties to a legal proceeding are governed by the law of the place where those rights arose.

MALUM IN SE: Evil or wrong in and of itself; inherently wrong. This term describes an act that is wrong by its very nature, as opposed to one which would not be wrong but for the fact that there is a specific legal prohibition against it (malum prohibitum).

MALUM PROHIBITUM: Wrong because prohibited, but not inherently evil. Used to describe something that is wrong because it is expressly forbidden by law but that is not in and of itself evil, e.g., speeding.

MANDAMUS: We command. A writ directing an official to take a certain action.

MENS REA: A guilty mind; a criminal intent. A term used to signify the mental state that accompanies a crime or other prohibited act. Some crimes require only a general mens rea (general intent to do the prohibited act), but others, like assault with intent to murder, require the existence of a specific mens rea.

MODUS OPERANDI: Method of operating; generally refers to the manner or style of a criminal in committing crimes, admissible in appropriate cases as evidence of the identity of a defendant.

NEXUS: A connection to.

NISI PRIUS: A court of first impression. A nisi prius court is one where issues of fact are tried before a judge or jury.

N.O.V. (NON OBSTANTE VEREDICTO): Notwithstanding the verdict. A judgment n.o.v. is a judgment given in favor of one party despite the fact that a verdict was returned in favor of the other party, the justification being that the verdict either had no reasonable support in fact or was contrary to law.

NUNC PRO TUNC: Now for then. This phrase refers to actions that may be taken and will then have full retroactive effect.

PENDENTE LITE: Pending the suit; pending litigation under way.

PER CAPITA: By head; beneficiaries of an estate, if they take in equal shares, take per capita.

PER CURIAM: By the court; signifies an opinion ostensibly written "by the whole court" and with no identified author.

PER SE: By itself, in itself; inherently.

PER STIRPES: By representation. Used primarily in the law of wills to describe the method of distribution where a person, generally because of death, is unable to take that which is left to him by the will of another, and therefore his heirs divide such property between them rather than take under the will individually.

PRIMA FACIE: On its face, at first sight. A prima facie case is one that is sufficient on its face, meaning that the evidence supporting it is adequate to establish the case until contradicted or overcome by other evidence.

PRO TANTO: For so much; as far as it goes. Often used in eminent domain cases when a property owner receives partial payment for his land without prejudice to his right to bring suit for the full amount he claims his land to be worth.

QUANTUM MERUIT: As much as he deserves. Refers to recovery based on the doctrine of unjust enrichment in those cases in which a party has rendered valuable services or furnished materials that were accepted and enjoyed by another under circumstances that would reasonably notify the recipient that the rendering party expected to be paid. In essence, the law implies a contract to pay the reasonable value of the services or materials furnished.

QUASI: Almost like; as if; nearly. This term is essentially used to signify that one subject or thing is almost analogous to another but that material differences between them do exist. For example, a quasi-criminal proceeding is one that is not strictly criminal but shares enough of the same characteristics to require some of the same safeguards (e.g., procedural due process must be followed in a parole hearing).

QUID PRO QUO: Something for something. In contract law, the consideration, something of value, passed between the parties to render the contract binding.

RES GESTAE: Things done; in evidence law, this principle justifies the admission of a statement that would otherwise be hearsay when it is made so closely to the event in question as to be said to be a part of it, or with such spontaneity as not to have the possibility of falsehood.

RES IPSA LOQUITUR: The thing speaks for itself. This doctrine gives rise to a rebuttable presumption of negligence when the instrumentality causing the injury was within the exclusive control of the defendant, and the injury was one that does not normally occur unless a person has been negligent.

RES JUDICATA: A matter adjudged. Doctrine which provides that once a court of competent jurisdiction has rendered a final judgment or decree on the merits, that judgment or decree is conclusive upon the parties to the case and prevents them from engaging in any other litigation on the points and issues determined therein.

RESPONDEAT SUPERIOR: Let the master reply. This doctrine holds the master liable for the wrongful acts of his servant (or the principal for his agent) in those cases in which the servant (or agent) was acting within the scope of his authority at the time of the injury.

STARE DECISIS: To stand by or adhere to that which has been decided. The common law doctrine of stare decisis attempts to give security and certainty to the law by following the policy that once a principle of law as applicable to a certain set of facts has been set forth in a decision, it forms a precedent which will subsequently be followed, even though a different decision might be made were it the first time the question had arisen. Of course, stare decisis is not an inviolable principle and is departed from in instances where there is good cause (e.g., considerations of public policy led the Supreme Court to disregard prior decisions sanctioning segregation).

SUPRA: Above. A word referring a reader to an earlier part of a book.

ULTRA VIRES: Beyond the power. This phrase is most commonly used to refer to actions taken by a corporation that are beyond the power or legal authority of the corporation.

Addendum of French Derivatives

IN PAIS: Not pursuant to legal proceedings.

CHATTEL: Tangible personal property.

CY PRES: Doctrine permitting courts to apply trust funds to purposes not expressed in the trust but necessary to carry out the settlor's intent.

PER AUTRE VIE: For another's life; during another's life. In property law, an estate may be granted that will terminate upon the death of someone other than the grantee.

PROFIT A PRENDRE: A license to remove minerals or other produce from land.

VOIR DIRE: Process of questioning jurors as to their predispositions about the case or parties to a proceeding in order to identify those jurors displaying bias or prejudice.

Casenote® Legal Briefs

Subject	Authors
Administrative Law	Breyer, Stewart, Sunstein, Vermeule & Herz
Administrative Law	Cass, Diver, Beermann & Freeman
Administrative Law	Funk, Shapiro & Weaver
Administrative Law	Mashaw, Merrill & Shane
Administrative Law	Strauss, Rakoff & Farina (Gellhorn & Byse)
Agency & Partnership	Hynes & Loewenstein
Antitrust	Pitofsky, Goldschmid & Wood
Antitrust	Sullivan, Hovenkamp & Schelanski
Bankruptcy	Warren & Bussel
Business Organizations	Allen, Kraakman & Subramanian
Business Organizations	Bauman, Weiss & Palmiter
Business Organizations	Hamilton & Macey
Business Organizations	Klein, Ramseyer & Bainbridge
Business Organizations	O'Kelley & Thompson
Business Organizations	Smiddy & Cunningham
Civil Procedure	Field, Kaplan & Clermont
Civil Procedure	Freer & Perdue
Civil Procedure	Friedenthal, Miller, Sexton & Hershkoff
Civil Procedure	Hazard, Tait, Fletcher & Bundy
Civil Procedure	Marcus, Redish, Sherman & Pfander
Civil Procedure	Subrin, Minow, Brodin & Main
Civil Procedure	Yeazell
Commercial Law	LoPucki, Warren, Keating & Mann
Commercial Law	Warren & Walt
Commercial Law	Whaley
Community Property	Bird
Community Property	Blumberg
Conflicts	Brilmayer, Goldsmith & O'Connor
Conflicts	Currie, Kay, Kramer & Roosevelt
Constitutional Law	Brest, Levinson, Balkin & Amar
Constitutional Law	Chemerinsky
Constitutional Law	Choper, Fallon, Kamisar & Shiffrin (Lockhart)
Constitutional Law	Cohen, Varat & Amar
Constitutional Law	Farber, Eskridge & Frickey
Constitutional Law	Rotunda
Constitutional Law	Sullivan & Gunther
Constitutional Law	Stone, Seidman, Sunstein, Tushnet & Karlan
Contracts	Ayres & Speidel
Contracts	Barnett
Contracts	Burton
Contracts	Calamari, Perillo & Bender
Contracts	Crandall & Whaley
Contracts	Dawson, Harvey, Henderson & Baird
Contracts	Farnsworth, Young, Sanger, Cohen & Brooks
Contracts	Fuller & Eisenberg
Contracts	Knapp, Crystal & Prince
Copyright	Cohen, Loren, Okediji & O'Rourke
Copyright, Patent, and Trademark	Goldstein & Reese
Criminal Law	Bonnie, Coughlin, Jeffries & Low
Criminal Law	Boyce, Dripps & Perkins
Criminal Law	Dressler
Criminal Law	Johnson & Cloud
Criminal Law	Kadish, Schulhofer & Steiker
Criminal Law	Kaplan, Weisberg & Binder
Criminal Procedure	Allen, Stuntz, Hoffman, Livingston & Leipold
Criminal Procedure	Dressler & Thomas
Criminal Procedure	Haddad, Marsh, Zagel, Meyer, Starkman & Bauer
Criminal Procedure	Kamisar, LaFave, Israel, King & Kerr
Criminal Procedure	Saltzburg & Capra
Debtors and Creditors	Warren & Westbrook
Employment Discrimination	Friedman
Employment Discrimination	Zimmer, Sullivan & White
Employment Law	Rothstein & Liebman
Environmental Law	Menell & Stewart
Environmental Law	Percival, Schroeder, Miller & Leape
Environmental Law	Plater, Abrams, Goldfarb, Graham, Heinzerling & Wirth
Evidence	Broun, Mosteller & Giannelli
Evidence	Fisher
Evidence	Mueller & Kirkpatrick
Evidence	Sklansky
Evidence	Waltz, Park & Friedman
Family Law	Areen & Regan
Family Law	Ellman, Kurtz, Weithorn, Bix, Czapanskiy & Eichner
Family Law	Harris, Carbone & Teitelbaum
Family Law	Wadlington & O'Brien
Family Law	Weisberg & Appleton
Federal Courts	Fallon, Meltzer & Shapiro (Hart & Wechsler)
Federal Courts	Low, Jeffries & Bradley
Health Law	Furrow, Greaney, Johnson, Jost & Schwartz
Immigration Law	Aleinikoff, Martin & Motomura
Immigration Law	Legomsky
Insurance Law	Abraham
Intellectual Property	Merges, Menell & Lemley
International Business Transactions	Folsom, Gordon, Spanogle & Fitzgerald
International Law	Blakesley, Firmage, Scott & Williams
International Law	Carter and Weiner
International Law	Damrosch, Henkin, Murphy & Smit
International Law	Dunoff, Ratner & Wippman
Labor Law	Cox, Bok, Gorman & Finkin
Land Use	Callies, Freilich & Roberts
Legislation	Eskridge, Frickey & Garrett
Oil & Gas	Lowe, Anderson, Smith & Pierce
Patent Law	Adelman, Radner, Thomas & Wegner
Products Liability	Owen, Montgomery & Davis
Professional Responsibility	Gillers
Professional Responsibility	Hazard, Koniak, Cramton, Cohen & Wendel
Property	Casner, Leach, French, Korngold & VanderVelde
Property	Cribbet, Johnson, Findley & Smith
Property	Donahue, Kauper & Martin
Property	Dukeminier, Krier, Alexander & Schill
Property	Haar & Liebman
Property	Kurtz & Hovenkamp
Property	Nelson, Stoebuck & Whitman
Property	Rabin, Kwall, Kwall & Arnold
Property	Singer
Real Estate	Korngold & Goldstein
Real Estate Transactions	Nelson & Whitman
Remedies	Laycock
Remedies	Shoben, Tabb & Janutis
Securities Regulation	Coffee, Seligman & Sale
Securities Regulation	Cox, Hillman & Langevoort
Sports Law	Weiler, Roberts, Abrams & Ross
Taxation (Corporate)	Lind, Schwartz, Lathrope & Rosenberg
Taxation (Individual)	Burke & Friel
Taxation (Individual)	Freeland, Lathrope, Lind & Stephens
Taxation (Individual)	Klein, Bankman, Shaviro & Stak
Torts	Dobbs, Hayden & Bublick
Torts	Epstein
Torts	Franklin, Rabin & Green
Torts	Henderson, Pearson, Kysar & Siliciano
Torts	Schwartz, Kelly & Partlett (Prosser)
Trademark	Ginsburg, Litman & Kevlin
Wills, Trusts & Estates	Dukeminier, Sitkoff & Lindgren
Wills, Trusts & Estates	Dobris, Sterk & Leslie
Wills, Trusts & Estates	Scoles, Halbach, Roberts & Begleiter